THE YOUTH WORKER'S GUIDE TO CREATIVE BIBLE STUDY

KAREN DOCKREY

VICTOR BOOKS®

A DIVISION OF SCRIPTURE PRESS PUBLICATIONS INC.
USA CANADA ENGLAND

Scripture references, unless otherwise indicated, are from the *Holy Bible, New International Version,* © 1973, 1978, 1984, International Bible Society. Used by permission of Zondervan Bible Publishers. Other quotations are from the *Authorized King James Version* (KJV) and the *Good News Bible* (GNB) — Old Testament: © American Bible Society 1976; New Testament: © American Bible Society 1966, 1971, 1976.

Library of Congress Cataloging-in-Publication Data

Dockrey, Karen, 1955 –
  The youth worker's guide to creative Bible study / by Karen Dockrey.
    p.   cm.
  ISBN 0-89693-548-5
  1. Bible – Study. 2. Church work with youth. I. Title.
BS600.2.D62 1991
220'.07 – dc20   90-23682
                                                    CIP

1 2 3 4 5 6 7 8 9 10 Printing/Year 95 94 93 92 91

C O N T E N T S

1
What Makes a Quality Bible Study?

Involvement Is the Key to Learning That Lasts

I don't see why we can't just teach the Bible. Why do we have to have all this "creative" stuff? I'm for serious Bible study. Youth should be too. "Serious Bible study" often means lecture and verse by verse "what-does-this-mean-to-you" Bible study. Valid as they are, these approaches are not the only ways to be serious about Bible study.

Teaching As Jesus Taught

I can think of no more serious teacher than Jesus Christ Himself. Look at the variety of ways He taught:*

1. *Jesus invited others to talk:* "Who do people say that I am?" Jesus invited talking by moving from general to specific, perhaps because people find it easier to begin talking about other people's opinions. Jesus then asked the personal question: "Who do *you* say I am?" (Matthew 16:15)

2. *Jesus asked questions:* Sometimes Jesus used questions to help people draw conclusions, such as when He spoke with the rich ruler about eternal life (Luke 18:18-29). Other times Jesus used questions to correct faulty thinking, as when He talked with religious leaders about authority (Matthew 21:23-27). Often Jesus did not answer His own questions but used them to lead His listeners toward truth.

3. *Jesus moved from the simple to the complex:* When Jesus talked with the woman at the well He began with water, compared that water to eternal life, and finally explained about the Messiah (John 4:1-26).

---

*Special thanks to Ron Moore for suggesting several of these methods.

4. Jesus compared spiritual truth to everyday experiences: Jesus' parables, "earthly stories with heavenly meaning," made spiritual truth clear. "The kingdom of God . . . is like a mustard seed" (Luke 13:19).

5. Jesus used assignments and challenges: He sent the disciples out in pairs to heal the sick and proclaim the kingdom of God. Notice the specificity of His instructions in Luke 10:1-12. He later challenged His followers to share His gospel with the world (Matthew 28:18-20).

6. Jesus taught by example: He served by washing His disciples' feet (John 13:1-7). He emphasized baptism by being baptized (Matthew 3:13-17). He respected people by taking time for children and by talking with ignored people (Matthew 19:14; John 4:9).

7. Jesus explained His examples: After washing His disciples' feet, Jesus urged them to express the same loving action (John 13:12-17).

8. Jesus befriended and accepted people: He spent time listening to and understanding people, regardless of their background. He accepted Zacchaeus, the hated tax collector, when no one else would. Rather than judging him, Jesus let God's love transform Zacchaeus (Luke 19:2-10).

9. Jesus gave evidence to end doubt: Rather than scolding Thomas for his religious questions, Jesus gave him the evidence he needed to believe (John 20:24-28).

10. Jesus quoted Scripture (Bible memory): Jesus defeated Satan's temptation with the Word (Matthew 4:1-11).

11. Jesus expressed emotion: He wept upon discovering Lazarus' death (John 11:35-36). He was angry with money changers in the temple (Mark 11:15-17). He agonized over His crucifixion (Luke 22:44).

12. Jesus responded to emotion: Jesus responded to His mother's worry by explaining why He stayed in the temple (Luke 2:49). Jesus comforted His disciples by assuring them He would prepare a place for them (John 14:1-3). At the Last Supper He tempered Peter's overconfidence by telling him what to do after failure (Luke 22:32).

13. Jesus forgave: After Peter denied Jesus, Jesus forgave Peter and challenged him to feed His sheep (John 21:16).

14. Jesus prayed for Himself and His students: With tenderness, compassion, and understanding of their challenges, Jesus prayed for His disciples, for all His followers, and for Himself (John 17).

15. Jesus affirmed correct conclusions: When Peter identified Jesus as "the Christ, the Son of the living God," Jesus confirmed his answer (Matthew 16:16-17).

16. *Jesus spent time with His students:* He called 12 people to be His closest disciples (Mark 1:17-20). He talked with them (Mark 11:20-25), rested with them (Mark 6:30-31), and shared the Last Supper with them (Mark 14:12-26). He also spent time teaching others who were interested in Him (Mark 6:34-44).

17. *Jesus gave object lessons:* He used a coin to teach about taxes (Mark 12:16-17). He used the stones of magnificent buildings to explain the intensity of the end of the age (Mark 13:1-4).

18. *Jesus used waiting and silence:* Jesus averted a potential catastrophe by waiting for would-be stoners to answer His question about sin (John 8:1-11). Jesus was silent before His accusers, perhaps realizing that words would do no good in that situation (Luke 23:9).

19. *Jesus gently but firmly corrected misunderstandings about God:* He helped His disciples see that children weren't a bother to "serious" religion, but a demonstration of it (Matthew 19:13-15). He rebuked His disciples when they spoke or acted wrongly (Mark 8:33).

20. *Jesus demonstrated truth:* Jesus walked on water to show God's power over nature and fear (Matthew 14:22-33). He ate with sinners to demonstrate that God wants everyone to come to Him (Matthew 9:11-12).

21. *Jesus used case studies:* He explained righteousness to the Pharisees with a story about two people in church (Luke 18:9-14).

22. *Jesus listened and encouraged others to listen:* He himself learned by listening to teachers in the temple (Luke 2:46). He reminded His followers to listen to understand (Matthew 11:15; 13:18; 15:10). God commanded people to listen to Jesus (Luke 9:35).

23. *Jesus made divine demands clear:* He commanded demons to leave innocent people (Luke 4:35). He expected His followers to obey God (John 14:23).

24. *Jesus admitted what He didn't know:* Jesus told His disciples that only God the Father knows the day and hour of Jesus' return (Mark 13:32).

25. *Jesus used lecture very occasionally:* The Sermon on the Mount (Matthew 5–7) is the one long lecture of Jesus recorded in the Bible.

No matter how Jesus taught, He guided His pupils to discover, understand, and live His truth. He involved them in the learning experience. What implications do Jesus' methods have for your teaching? How might you teach more like Jesus taught? Search

Matthew, Mark, Luke, John, and Acts 1:1-11 to study the way Jesus taught. Focus on Jesus as you plan Bible studies for your students.

Identify Good Bible Study Methods
I want to teach as Jesus did. But I don't want to end up entertaining youth rather than leading them to study the Bible. What's the difference between fun activities and solid Bible study?

Fun itself is not the measure of a good Bible study method; student involvement with the Bible is. When students read, search, and talk about the Bible, they learn. The "rationale" section at the beginning of chapters 4 through 13 shows how the ideas in each chapter will keep youth learning without losing interest.

Include Four Elements for Quality Bible Study
I feel better about trying new Bible study methods, but I'm not sure how to put a Bible study together. How do I arrange it?

A good Bible study is more than a conglomeration of methods. It's a meaningful progression of actions flowing from Bible fact discovery to Bible application. Most Bible study curricula will arrange this flow for you. When they don't, or when you're designing your own study, include four elements:

1. Read the Bible passage: Begin by giving youth a reason to read the Bible passage. Perhaps you'll challenge them to find the answer to a question or the names of certain Bible characters. Perhaps you'll ask them to place facts in order. Maybe they'll act out the passage, using the Bible as their script. Often the Bible fact assignment (element 2) is the motivation for reading the Bible.

2. Discover Bible facts: Without facts youth have no basis on which to make comments or draw conclusions. Guide them to discover Bible facts with a method like those described in chapters 5, 6, or 7. Perhaps they'll find a question under their chair that guides them to a fact. Maybe they'll create quizzes for each other and learn twice: once while writing the questions and again while answering.

3. Understand Bible facts: Guide your students to understand the facts they discover with a method from chapters 6–11. Understanding has two elements: (a) What the Bible facts meant to those in Bible times and (b) what the Bible facts mean to us today. Perhaps youth will illustrate sanctification by modeling with clay. Maybe they'll draw a "before-and-after" cartoon on the difference sanctification makes.

4. Apply the Bible to life: Close with a step that guides youth to live Bible truth. Bible knowledge means little if it never transforms lives. See the application methods in chapters 11–13. Perhaps your youth will write and mail a letter requesting forgiveness.

As you prepare and teach, you may find that these elements overlap. Your Bible-reading method may get kids asking questions about the facts in the passage. The fact method may guide youth to tell how that truth has worked in their lives. This is the way it should be: a meaningful flow rather than sharply defined steps.

If you refer to the table of contents, you will see that this book is organized around the above four elements of Bible study to make it easier for you to design a Bible study or help you discover an alternate method if your curriculum has a weak step.

Involvement: For Learning that Lasts

Every word in this chapter points to one concept: INVOLVEMENT. The ultimate goal of Bible study is to involve youth with God so they will trust Him as Saviour and follow Him as Lord. To guide youth to become involved with the Bible and thus with God:

• **Involve rather than inform:** Suppose you had climbed a mountain and wanted to convey to your students the exhilaration of reaching the top and the relief at discovering that the grueling work was really worth the effort. Would it be better to tell them about your climb or take them to the top of the mountain with you? Taking them to the top would take more time than saying: "The results are worth the climb." But which would impact their lives more deeply? It's the same with Bible study: the more youth do for themselves, the more meaningful their learning becomes.

• **Listen rather than lecture:** The one who talks is the one who learns. When you ask questions and make assignments that guide youth to express Bible understanding, they learn. It's easy to let lectures go in one ear and out the other, but youth remember what they themselves say. They live what they commit to.

• **Direct rather than dictate:** "Is this television program good for me?" "What is sin?" "How can I know the will of God?" Rather than telling youth what to do, guide them to Bible verses that address their questions. As youth make their own choices, they gain confidence in their ability to read, understand, and live the Bible for themselves. And they grow close to God who authored the Bible.

2
The Youth We Teach

When We Understand Youth, It Is More Likely
That They'll Understand the Bible

Teenagers have three predominant needs when they come to Bible
study: to feel safe, to look smart, and to discover how to be spiritual.
These needs are rooted in their moving from the dependence of
childhood to the independence of adulthood. They continually feel the
tension between wanting to be competent, likeable, and Christian,
but not quite making it. They want to try, but they fear failing. They
want to be honest, but they fear not being liked. They want to be
spiritual, but they aren't sure how—so they smile all the time, talk
with heavenly lingo, deny their struggles, and feel guilty. Jesus is the
answer to their three basic needs. Your actions in class can make it
easier for your students to recognize this.

Understand Their Needs

Begin by understanding that talking about spiritual things is hard. It
requires your students to reveal themselves and their very personal
relationship with God (or lack of relationship). To feel safe and smart
talking about such sacred things, they first have to feel safe and
smart talking about simple things. They must see how the Bible
relates to their worries and problems. They must have success with
answering Bible questions and opportunities to explore how spiritual
truth impacts life.

Make It Safe

The need for security plus youth's increased need for acceptance
make a safe Bible study setting crucial. Every day at school, home,
and work teenagers are criticized and put down. They need a haven

from the cruelty of the world—a place where they can talk and feel and wonder and ask, without a hint of ridicule. Provide a place where every question is respected and where the entire class works together to find God's answers to life's problems. This kind of loving gives youth a glimpse of heaven, a glimpse of the way God loves.

To make your class safe:

● Show interest in and listen to youth's everyday concerns. "How was school?" "How are things at home?" "How's your love life?" "Tell me about that job interview." "What's happening in your friendships?"

● Introduce a class rule that no one may laugh at anyone else's comment, question, or concern. "No question is a dumb question, and every comment makes sense when you hear what's really said. We'll listen to each other and not laugh at each other under any circumstance."

Make Them Smart with Bible Success

All except those few school-smart kids will be afraid of looking stupid in front of their peers and in front of you. Even the school-smart will be cautious about looking too smart or may not know their Bible as well as their algebra. To keep from looking dumb, students will cut up, pretend they didn't hear the question, refuse to participate, or deliberately act stupid.

Meet all youth's need to look smart by structuring the session so they have success with the Bible. Begin with questions that come directly from Scripture and proceed to application. Guide youth to succeed in small ways so they'll venture the more difficult questions. Show them that their attempts to answer spiritual questions will be accepted even when they're not quite right, and that people won't laugh when they try. As youth grow to trust their ability to read and understand the Bible, they'll turn to it more frequently for advice, comfort, and answers.

To help youth be smart:

● Begin with the easier questions and move toward harder ones. When Jesus talked with His disciples after His resurrection, He began by asking about their feelings: "Why are you troubled?" (Luke 24:38) He then asked another easy question: "Do you have anything to eat?" (Luke 24:41) He ended by explaining deep spiritual truths (Luke 24:44-49).

● Provide an answer source. Guide youth to open to the Bible passage before you start asking questions. Or direct them to the place in the student book that explains the assignment you give.

● Make your directions very specific. Rather than, "Write the passage in your own words" say, "Write the verse down with a blank line between each line. Then change the situations and names to ones that could happen today."

● Notice success. "You did great on that one!" "Thanks for contributing." "Without you this class wouldn't go nearly as well." "Very good answer on a hard question." The more youth succeed with the Bible, the more they'll trust themselves to read and under- and it and the more readily they'll turn to it at home. Choose methods that stretch youth—but not so far that they can't succeed.

Make It Spiritual

When youth feel safe and smart, they begin to share their deepest needs. As they share those needs, they find that God is the One to meet them. They discover that security and success are based in God. They discover that talking honestly with God empowers them to handle struggles and solve problems, that guilt means not that they are bad but that they need to examine themselves, and that giving in to temptation—not temptation itself—is sin. They realize that spirituality is a natural expression of their relationship with God.

To encourage spiritual growth:

● Guide youth to specific actions that express their growing spirituality. For example, help youth recognize guilt in their lives and the steps of confession, and repentance. Rejoice over temptations they have resisted that week. Invite them to share new ways they have obeyed God recently. Guide youth to discover that spirituality is a steering wheel, not a spare tire.

● Present spirituality as a journey and a series of choices rather than as something you have or don't have. Too many people see their salvation decision as the only decision they ever need to make for Jesus. Guide them to discover that they make daily decisions for or against Jesus. When they talk to a friend, do they decide to love her as Jesus does or cut her down as the world does? When they have a problem, do they choose to redeem the situation or get revenge? When they feel guilty, do they decide to change the behavior that caused it or let it destroy them?

● Continually point to Jesus as the source of answers and solutions. As youth understand that Jesus has been through it all, cares about them, and really does understand their worries, they turn to Him for answers. Point out why and how Jesus' ways work.

Meet Other Youth Needs

The above three needs—to be safe, smart, and spiritual—are rooted in the rapid changes youth undergo between puberty and adulthood. They grow physically, psychologically, socially, cognitively, and morally in dramatic ways. During this crucial time, youth have tremendous need for success, for acceptance by peers, for understanding from adults, for development of mature faith, for growth of identity as a child of God, and for courage to keep faith commitments. Quality Bible teaching can equip youth for these and other growth needs.

The following list summarizes developmental characteristics of youth. As you read the insights of Gesell and Erikson, ponder teaching methods that could address these characteristics.

The Identity Stage of Youth (Erikson)

● **Temporal perspective versus time confusion:** How do I relate to the past, the future, the present? What does my future hold?

● **Self-certainty versus self-consciousness:** Do they like me? Can I succeed when I try?

● **Role experimentation versus role fixation:** Which roles, ideas, and personality are best for me? How can I avoid being two-faced or hypocritical?

● **Apprenticeship versus work paralysis:** What do I want to be when I grow up? Which of my interests could become a satisfying job?

● **Sexual polarization versus bisexual confusion:** How can I be comfortable relating to the opposite sex? What is God's purpose for my sexual feelings?

● **Leadership versus authority confusion:** When, where, and with whom am I capable of leading? Whom must I follow?

● **Ideological commitment versus confusion of values:** What are my ideals and commitments? How do I act when my values and commitments are challenged?

(List reprinted from the kit *Youth Challenge: Sunday School Outreach,* by Karen Dockrey, © 1985 Convention Press. All rights reserved. Used by permission.)

Biological Growth (Gesell)

- Progress, regression, and then progress again.
- Sometimes well-adjusted, confident, reasonable, outgoing, balanced.
- Sometimes moody, restless, rebellious, quarrelsome, withdrawn, sensitive, critical, and self-conscious.
- Girls one-and-a-half to two years ahead of boys.
- Some youth mature earlier or later than the norm.

"And my God will meet all your needs according to His glorious riches in Christ Jesus" (Philippians 4:19).

Address Needs of Youth

As you select teaching methods, ask yourself how they address the developmental needs of your specific youth. Of course youth are individuals, but all youth struggle in some way with the needs discussed in the previous section. The following examples suggest ways to address each of these needs. Notice that many activities could meet more than one need:

- "Human Tic-Tac-Toe" (chapter 5) can meet youth's need for success because no one has to miss a question for the game to work.
- "Cued Reading" (chapter 4) meets the need for acceptance because it shows that many people struggle with understanding certain Scripture verses—youth feel part of the group.
- "Agree/Disagree" (chapter 8) helps youth understand their beliefs by voicing every aspect of them. As youth talk about their faith, their faith grows deeper and more personal.
- "Dilemmas" and "Pretend You Are There" (chapter 13) guide youth to discover how faith applies to life because they must voice what they would do in the specific circumstance.
- "Popular Tunes" (chapter 12) helps make faith personal because as youth sing the Scripture they remember to live it.
- Clay Shaping" (chapter 9) helps youth talk about their faith by giving a prop for demonstrating and explaining complex truths.
- "Paper Cup Shaping" and "Tangram" (chapter 9) help youth with their progress, regression, and then progress again because they can speak from where they are developmentally.
- Any talking method (chapter 8) enhances the well-adjusted, confident, reasonable, outgoing, balanced side of youth.
- "Affirmation" (chapter 13) tames the moody, restless, rebel-

lious, quarrelsome, withdrawn, sensitive, critical and self-conscious side of youth by helping them feel loved for who they are.

● Studying any Old or New Testament passage helps youth with temporal perspective by relating to the past and the present. Youth can relate to the future by studying Mark 13 and Revelation.

● "Walk and Find" (chapter 6) helps youth mingle with others and grow in certainty by discovering "direct-from-the-passage" answer.

● "Role Play" (chapter 9) helps youth discover and practice their role as Christians (role experimentation) and the role they'd like to hold in the occupational world (apprenticeship).

● Being with the opposite sex in class helps youth become comfortable with and know persons of the opposite sex (sexual polarization).

● Any team work (all chapters, but especially chapters 5, 11, and 13) helps youth develop leadership and respect for each another.

● "What If I Do/What If I Don't" (chapter 9) gives youth courage to keep faith commitments by addressing the consequences of obeying or disobeying God's commandments. It enables youth to "dress rehearse" decisions before they have to make actual ones (ideological commitment).

The Big B: Boredom

Another need of youth, seldom addressed in literature, is stimulation. Youth bore easily. Part of it is because of our quick paced, highly visual society. More of it is because youth need meaningful learning. Face it: We all get bored, but youth are more honest about it—adults smile and look interested when their minds are miles away. Youth let you know when the learning doesn't meet their needs.

Until youth are old enough to attach meaning to Bible learning, we do it for them. The Bible is intriguing, need-meeting, and life-changing. Help your students see this by consciously showing how each passage applies to life, answers a life question, or makes it easier to love and trust God. Ways to do this include:

● **Provide multiple options.** Youth, like persons of all ages, like to learn in different ways. Take advantage of their diversity by offering at least two response options with every assignment: draw or write, say or sing, act or describe, list or doodle. As students express Bible truth in ways that are comfortable to them, learning takes on meaning.

● **Discover and use what your students like best.** If you have doodlers, focus on art methods (chapter 9). If your group talks incessantly, choose talking methods (chapter 8). If one youth monopolizes the class, choose methods for which all youth have to respond (chapters 6, 7, 8). If your youth ham it up, use drama (chapter 9). Notice that each chapter includes at least 10 variations. If your youth have, as most classes do, a variety of interests, vary your methods. While focusing on your students' favorites, remember to stretch them with new experiences. Learning-style research indicates that we all learn best with a variety of learning styles.

• **Use variety in every element of teaching.** Variety stimulates youth's curiosity and gives them new ways to understand Scripture. Vary your room setup by arranging chairs in the shape of a heart when talking about love or by taking the chairs out completely when talking about Peter's imprisonment. Change your visuals weekly to match the theme of the study. Then when youth's eyes wander, the visual will bring them back to the subject. Vary how youth learn Bible facts by using scavenger hunts, placing facts in order, finding the mistake, learning games, and more. Put questions under chairs, in a bag, or give the answer and get the question. Scan chapters 4–13 when you find yourself in a teaching rut.

• **Obviously value everything youth say, make, and share.** Listen attentively to youth. Invite them to be a part of the teaching by finding a contemporary Christian song for your theme, by setting up the chairs, writing dilemmas, creating posters. Always display their creations.

• **Take youth seriously enough to do serious Bible study.** Entertaining youth is meaningless because it is not connected to the real answer: Jesus Christ. Discover and use teaching methods that take youth deeply into the Bible and guide them to explore it with fascination and commitment. Involve; don't entertain.

The Way I See Me

Self-esteem may be the most crucial adolescent need because the way youth view themselves impacts the way they view God and the way they love others.

Youth with high self-esteem find it easier to believe God loves them. They feel more confident about reading and interpreting the Bible and doing what the Bible says. They see Bible commands as pointers toward happiness, not prohibitions of fun.

Youth with low self-esteem find it hard to believe God loves them.

They hesitate to read the Bible because they're certain they won't understand it anyway. They hesitate to obey God's commands because they fear failing and incurring God's wrath. They see Bible commands as proof of their personal inadequacy. They're certain the way to win God's favor is to be good; something they don't think they can do.

You can help meet your students' needs for self-esteem by genuinely loving them. Youth tend to equate your love with God's love because you represent the church. Show your love by saying their names, by listening to their stories, by inviting their insights.

You can also further self-esteem by giving plentiful opportunity for genuine success with the Bible. Choose methods that point to specific Bible passages, that encourage each youth to talk and share, and that offer multiple response options (draw or write, etc.).

Finally, meet self-esteem needs by noticing when youth do well and giving genuine compliments. It's nearly impossible to give youth a big head. "Sunday just wasn't Sunday without you here." "Brilliant answer—we're lucky to have you." "I never thought of it quite that way—what keen insight—I'm impressed!" "Your smile looks especially nice today." Under no circumstances put down a young person. Sarcasm is not sarcasm to youth; it's proof you don't like them. Use your words to show youth that you and God genuinely value them.

God is on youth's side. Let everything you do and say during Bible study communicate that. Draw them nearer and nearer to the One who can meet their every need—God Himself.

Focus on Your Age Group's Needs

The first portion of this chapter has addressed needs of all youth. How do these needs vary among younger and older youth? Generally speaking, older youth like more discussion and younger youth like more movement. Older youth deal better with abstractions and principles, whereas younger youth want facts and black-and-white answers. Older youth are more willing to risk talking, contributing, and sharing than are younger youth.

Though greater variations exist within age groups than between them, these generalities can help you understand your specific youth and pick just the right Bible teaching method for them.

Younger Youth

Younger youth—those in junior high or middle school—are just beginning to move from childhood to adulthood. You'll see glimpses of childishness followed by a desperate but unspoken plea to be treated as mature. Junior highers are delighted to be in the youth group and will try almost anything simply because it's a "youth" activity. Because they so desperately want to be grown up, make a point to seriously call them "men" and "women." Avoid the label "children."

Junior highers are delightful because of their gregariousness. They love to be together and will come to Bible study simply because their friends come. This has great implications for evangelism because junior highers will come to church like no other age group. Their ability to understand abstract concepts is growing, so they are ready to make a lifelong commitment to Jesus Christ. Junior highers are eager to live for Jesus, especially if their friends are living for Jesus. Junior highers are a tremendous tribute to the positive impact peer pressure can have.

Junior highers are still moderately committed to pleasing the teacher. Thus your expectations will have a great effect on them. Expect good insight, clear understanding, and loving words, and you will usually receive them. Let the class know you'd like to build a loving group and guide them to do so with affirmation times, sharing prayer needs and answers, and jointly sending notes to those who miss class or are going through rough times.

Because junior highers exhibit tremendous energy, they need the safety of your limits. They need your loving tolerance, your consistency, and your self-discipline. They need to know what's expected of them and how to do it. Explain that if they work hard on their Bible study challenges, you will reward them with five minutes of free talking time. Insist that they be good to one another by giving compliments rather than cuts. Guide them to listen to each other because every person's opinion is an important one. Junior highers need you to keep an ordered classroom where opinions can be expressed without ridicule. Until junior highers can develop their own self-discipline, they need yours.

Junior highers are beginning to think abstractly but feel safer with direct-from-the-Bible-or-commentary answers. Spend more time with facts and direct answers than with generalities and principles. Don't neglect application, but parallel it closely to the passage you are studying.

Junior highers want to participate in meaningful ministry but may not know how. Help them know what to say in a note to a family with a tragedy. Invite a junior higher along while you visit for your church.

Guide them to share each other's joys and sadness. Schedule funeral home or hospital visits so junior highers know when to go and how long to stay.

Junior highers need your loving attention. They'll want you to listen to their stories, hear their successes, sympathize with their failures. Make it a point to arrive early for Bible study, so you can chat as youth arrive.

Junior highers tend to like:
- Bible studies on relationships like friendship, family, romance;
- Learning games with answers directly from the Scripture;
- Puzzles;
- Decoding;
- Staying in one group;
- "Hot Bag" (chapter 8);
- Filling in Sunday cartoons (chapter 7) and creating cartoons (9);
- Fast-paced, frequently changed activities;
- Applying the Bible to real problems.

Junior highers tend to shy away from:
- Highly abstract discussions;
- Putting truth into their own words unless directions are very specific;
- Answering questions not directly from Scripture or the commentary;
- Too much sitting and talking.

Older Youth
Older youth—in high school or older—are closer to adulthood than to childhood. Many have grown physically as much as they will grow. Don't let their mature bodies fool you into thinking they have it all together. Though older youth want independence, they need to know that it is OK to struggle, to wonder, to get help from others. Treat your senior highers as the mature people they are while allowing them the security of not being in charge. Sharing your own struggles will free senior highers to share their fears of growing up and making responsible choices. Then together you can find ways to make those choices.

Senior highers have more independence, thanks to a driver's license and at least part-time use of a car. Many have jobs or other commitments that keep them away from Bible study. Try not to lose touch with these youth: send them the student sheet of the study they missed. Telephone or write youth who come to Bible studies to thank them for their attendance and an insightful contribution they made.

Find out which youth have become Christians and which have not. Make a point to pray for and look for opportunities to share Christ with those who have not. Many of those who do not become Christians by high school graduation are lost forever.

Senior highers want to be respected by their Bible study teachers, and they want to respect their teachers. This mutual respect is enhanced when you listen to them as carefully as you want to be listened to, when you affirm insights they make, when you maintain a class that focuses on Bible study rather than deteriorates into chaos. Let the class know you want to build a loving group whose members encourage each other to grow in Christ. Guide them to affirm the good they see in others and to consciously involve each other in class activities. Explain that much of Christianity is deliberate loving action, motivated by obedience to Jesus.

Senior highers need you to go deep. Don't be afraid to delve into issues with no easy answers, such as why bad things happen to good people or why good things happen to bad people. If you don't know the answer, don't be afraid to say so. Invite youth to share their ideas with biblical support. Research any questions you cannot answer.

Older youth want to grasp and understand abstract concepts. Move more quickly from facts to concepts and conclusions than you would with younger youth. For example: When studying the loaves and the fishes (Mark 6:30-44), younger youth will understand *sharing* as an application. Older youth can expand to *"My little contribution combined with God's power brings great results."*

Interestingly, older youth tend to be more open to trying activities sometimes classified as "babyish" (clay molding, acting, putting the truth into one sentence) because they aren't as concerned as younger youth about looking mature. They will amaze you with the depth of spiritual insight they express in these activities.

Senior highers need you to admit that the world is not perfect. Not all parents consider their children's needs. Not all bosses are fair. Not all Christians act like Christians. This imperfect world is countered by a very perfect Saviour and Guide, Jesus Christ. Affirm that following Jesus won't take away all problems but will certainly minimize them. Emphasize that obeying Jesus is the best alternative to the inconsistency of this world.

Senior highers want to participate in meaningful ministry, often wanting to choose those ministries themselves. Respond to their ideas, help them determine motive and purpose, and guide them through the detail work that makes ministry successful. Cultivate the habit of daily ministry by brainstorming ways to minister at work and school. Apprentice them by inviting them along as you do ministry.

Like junior highers, senior highers need your loving attention. They'll want your pride when they resist temptation, your prayer for relationships, your help with decisions (do more listening than talking and more pointing to Bible verses than giving pat answers). Make it a point to arrive early for Bible study and be ready, so you can chat as youth arrive.

Senior highers tend to like:
- Bible studies on relationships like friendship, family, romance;
- Word searches;
- Putting truth into their own words (such as "Life Motto," chapter 13);
- Learning games with some answers directly from the Scripture and some very hard questions;
- Sculpting and sharing abstract subjects;
- Team challenges that have obvious meaning;
- Debates;
- Hard issues to which they can all express their ideas;
- Applying the Bible to real problems.

Senior highers tend to shy away from:
- Decoding;
- Fill-in-the-blanks unless it is words to a song;
- True/false unless there is both true and falsehood in each statement and they must find the deception;
- Activities that seem meaningless. They want to know why they're doing it. For instance, explain that the "Trading Game" (chapter 5) helps them memorize several elements of a particular truth.

3
Ten Commandments for Guiding a Youth Bible Study

How You Use Methods Is as Important as Using Methods

A good Bible teaching method involves youth in the Bible. Youth's spiritual growth through Bible learning, not creativity for creativity's sake, is our goal.

I. Thou Shalt Teach with Enthusiasm and Expectation

If you like Bible study, your students will tend to like it also. If you present a learning activity with interest and expectation, youth will participate and like it. But if you say, "This was in the book and I know you will think it's childish and dumb . . . " they will think it's childish and dumb. Expect great insight based on Bible truths. Your students will sense your expectation and fulfill it.

II. Thou Shalt Involve Every Youth in Bible Study

When was the last time you stole Bible learning from your teenagers? Of course you wouldn't do this intentionally, but consider that the one who does the talking, searching, and thinking is the one who learns. How often have you reserved this privilege for yourself by studying during the week and then pouring out your knowledge for your pupils? Avoid this temptation by choosing a few methods each week that involve every youth in meaningful Bible searching, interpreting, and living. Guide them to discover God's truths for themselves. Youth involvement is the key to learning that lasts.

III. Thou Shalt Give Youth a Reason to Read the Bible

Too often we read the Bible in unison or one-person-to-a-verse and then "get down to the serious Bible study." When we begin asking questions, we notice that our students have to read the passage again. The first reading didn't even register. Why not let the Bible question or assignment be youth's motivation to read the Bible? When we give the question first, youth read the passage with purpose, seeking to find answers. Sample challenges include:

- Look for Jesus' view of faith and works in James 2:14-26.
- Read the passage to find the answers to the game.
- As you read, notice the character that is most like you and why.

IV. Thou Shalt Give an Answer Source

When you ask a question or make an assignment, let your students know where to find the answer in the Bible. This keeps them from generalizing or drawing on past knowledge. When you give a definite passage to read, you show that the Bible has definite answers to today's question. Consider these examples:

- Write three guidelines for how a Christian should view money. Search 1 Timothy 6:1-10 for ideas.
- When is it right to limit your freedom for the sake of someone else's spiritual growth? If you know it is right, is it OK to do it regardless of the situation? Search 1 Corinthians 8:1-13 for ideas.

V. Thou Shalt Add a "Why?" Or "How?"

Refuse to settle for the standard "church answers." ("Go to church;" "Read your Bible." "Pray." "Love one another." "Witness.") Help youth discover not only *what* God wants them to do but specifically *how* and *why*. Move them to practical application with prompters like:

- "Give me an example of how to do that."
- "What could you say to make it happen?"
- "What action would show you believe that?"
- "How have you seen that happen at your school/home?"

When youth can tell you the reason for God's rule, they understand that rule and tend to obey it. When youth can give an example of how to live a Bible truth, they know how to live it. When youth can describe or express their relationship with God, they grow closer to Him. When youth discover that God's ways bring the greatest happiness, they are more likely to enjoy Him.

VI. Thou Shalt Encourage Youth to Talk

The one who talks is the one who learns. So let your students talk more than you do. Guide pre-Bible study chatter to focus on the

Bible passage and theme. Use methods from chapters 6 (asking questions) and 8 (encouraging discussion) to motivate involvement.

IMPORTANT: Saying something does not necessarily mean believing it. Students may be voicing a view they heard someone else say. They may be trying out one of God's ideas to see how it will work. Listen, understand, and gently guide them to compare what they say to what God's Word says. For example: Jason reacted against "Obey your parents" (Ephesians 6:1). Rather than, "Who are you to question God's Word!" his teacher said, "You must have a good reason to react so strongly. Tell me why you feel that way." Honest discussion demonstrated that Jason's dad had abused Jason's sister and wanted Jason to keep it a secret. Jason rightly concluded that he should not obey this request.

VII. Thou Shalt Welcome Every Answer

It takes tremendous courage for most teenagers to speak up in class. When they try, make them glad they did. For right answers, respond with, "Good job! You're right on target!" For partially right answers, try; "You're on the right track. What else does verse 23 say about that?" For totally off-the-wall answers, try something like, "I'm pleased that you spoke up. This is a hard question and your answer is one many people give. How does verse 30 give a different way of thinking about it?" For dangerously wrong answers, try something like, "I don't agree with your conclusion because God's Word says _____ and that conclusion would hurt people by _____. What other conclusion might you draw?"

Each time students' answers are welcomed, they feel welcomed and stay involved with the study. If their contributions are laughed at, rejected, or ridiculed, youth will withdraw, cease to learn, and feel they're failures at Christianity.

Every time your students find a Bible answer correctly, interpret a passage well, or make a wise point in class, they gain confidence in their own ability to read and understand and live the Bible for themselves. Success comes with keeping Bibles open, starting with obvious questions and moving to harder ones, welcoming every answer, and giving clear directions. Success with the Bible is your goal.

VIII. Thou Shalt Never Answer Thine Own Question

Silently count to 10 after asking questions. Resist the temptation to answer your own question if your students take "too long." Because you have been thinking about the question since you prepared the lesson, the answer is on the tip of your tongue. Your students have just heard it and need some time to think about it. If after 20 seconds no one answers, rephrase the question or give a more specific verse to look in.

IX. Thou Shalt Affirm Ways Youth Live Their Faith

More than any other age group, teenagers doubt themselves. They worry about their salvation. They wonder if people like them. They hesitate to live their faith for fear they will let God down. Every time you notice and point out a way a student lives out his faith, you give him confidence to live it again. Your attention encourages your students to trust God and grow close to Him. Statements that affirm and increase faith actions include:

- "I like the way you welcomed Meghan today."
- "That answer showed real insight!"
- "You thought of something I hadn't. Thanks for helping me grow!"
- "The adults have been bragging on the way you guys have fun in good ways. I'm really proud of your testimony for Christ. You show that Christians really do have more fun!"

X. Thou Shalt Love Your Students and Yourself

Youth frequently equate your love for them with God's love. Make it a point to speak to each student every time you are together, to send notes about the good things they do in class, to let them know they are very important to God and to you. Treat your youth like the almost-adults they are. As you take youth seriously, they'll take you, your Bible study, and your Saviour seriously.

Part of loving your students is taking good care of yourself as a teacher. As you work with your youth you may become frustrated, exhilarated, defeated, and triumphant all in the same day. These pains and pleasures of working with youth become less painful and more pleasurable when you:

- Learn along with your students. There's no need to return to an adult class to learn. Take care of your own learning by participating in learning projects with your students. Fill out and share the worksheets, make that confession, say that speech, grade yourself. Be excited about new discoveries.
- Grow along with students. Let your class know what you

learned while preparing to teach. Share your struggles to love people (no names, of course), to understand a difficult spiritual principle, to resist a temptation. Feel free to say, "I'm not sure" or, "I'd better think about that one." Let your students know when they give you a new insight. All this teaches that Christianity is a journey, a pilgrimage, a never-ending adventure of new discoveries and steady growth toward Christlikeness.

● Find at least one other teacher you can talk with about teaching youth. Youth work is both exasperating and delightful. You need someone with whom to share both. Best is another youth teacher, but if you are the only youth teacher, find a teacher of another age group. Anyone who teaches will share your joy of breaking through to a student who had ignored you before, of seeing someone participate who felt shy before, or of watching a student make a decision to follow Christ in a new area. Another teacher will understand your frustration when you prepare but forget your main point, share your broken heart when one student ridicules another, rejoice with you when a student accepts Jesus Christ as Saviour.

Enjoy youth and take them seriously. See the good in them and let them know what you see (Philemon 4–7). Let God love youth through you and love you through youth. Realize that your work with youth can change lives—both yours and the youth with whom you work.

4
Read the Bible in a Way That Sticks

Make Bible-Reading Purposeful and Memorable

Rationale: We must read the Bible to know what it says. But too often Bible-reading becomes a dull, routine preliminary to the rest of the lesson. Students may barely attend to the passage because they've "heard it so many times." Before they begin reading, challenge students to discover specific facts from the passage, then vary the way they do the reading itself. This chapter suggests activities to help youth see the Bible as the fascinating and exciting Book it is.

Teaching Tip: Encourage youth to bring their own Bibles by using Bibles during every Bible study and by affirming those who bring them. If your curriculum includes printed Scripture, use it sparingly, such as when an activity requires all to have the same translation. As youth use their own Bibles, they locate passages, mark them, personalize them, use them.

BIBLE AS SCRIPT

Explain to your students that one of the best ways to understand Bible characters is to reenact events in their lives. Challenge each youth to discover how his or her character felt and what the character might say about the experience. Assign each youth a role from the passage (choose passages with crowds or plural parts so everyone has a part) and guide them to act it out, using their Bible for a script. Rather than using a narrator, instruct youth to read their actions as well as words.

Because youth will likely not have looked at the passage beforehand, direct each element of the drama by moving them into position, by pointing out turns, by praising their good work.

ADAPTATION: Provide name tags for each part.

HINT: If your curriculum includes printed Scripture, highlight the verses for each part.

Effective passages for acting include:

- Parable of the Sower (Youth play the parts of seeds and the farmer.)
- Parable of the Weeds (Youth play weeds, the sower, the enemy, the owner's servants, the harvesters.)
- Parable of the Vinegrowers (Youth like pretending to beat and kill one another. They are then amazed to discover that is the way prophets and Jesus were treated.)
- Any of Jesus' parables
- The baptism of Jesus (Matthew 3:13-17) (Interview the watching crowd afterward to ask their reactions to Jesus baptism and why it occurred.)
- Old Testament passages with lots of drama.

BIBLE MARKING

Guide youth to read the passage and mark it with symbols. Encourage them to write (in pencil) in their own Bibles or the one borrowed from your department. Distribute copies of the passage to any who are uncomfortable writing in their Bibles. Use three or four symbols at most, choosing from these samples:

o : circle what you like

? : question what puzzles you

x : cross out what you need to remove from your life

↻ : point to the actions you want to take

— : underline actions you want to avoid

= : put an equal sign by commands you're already obeying

! : exclaim over what makes you feel good about God

Let the marking lead you naturally into talking about the passage. Students can share what puzzles them (?) and others can suggest how they understand that passage. Supplement with Bible commentary. Students can share what they like (o,!) in the passage. This encourages and reminds youth that they always understand some of a passage.

CUED READING

This method is especially effective with passages with big words or complex truths because it draws attention to main concepts or confusing words. Follow the reading with a "Word Study" (chapter 11) or some other explanatory step.

To do a cued reading:

1. Write a copy of your passage with group responses in it, as in the following example.

2. Prepare a cue card for each response.

3. Enlist youth cue-card holders and seat them at the front with a copy of the cued passage.

4. Instruct youth to listen as you read the passage and do as the cue cards say. As you read the passage, card holders cue the audience. This example is from 2 Timothy 1:8-9 (GNB).

> Do not be ashamed [HUH?] then, of witnessing for our Lord [OH!]; neither be ashamed of me, a prisoner [HUH?]. Instead, take your part in suffering for the Good News, [HUH?] as God gives you strength for it. [OH!]
>
> He saved us and called us to be His own people [CHEER] not because of what we have done [OH!], but because of His own purpose and grace [CHEER].

FILL IN THE BLANK

Print a copy of your Scripture passage with key words replaced by blanks. Invite one student to read the passage while others fill in the blanks. This encourages youth to listen for and focus on key concepts. Use the key words for your "Understand the Bible Facts" step (see chapters 6–10 for ideas).

FIND IT

Challenge youth to find and mark certain details in the passage that will focus them on the truth you want to teach. For example:

- Circle every use of the word "all" in Deuteronomy 6:4-5. Which "all" would be easiest for you? Hardest for you? How do you love God thoroughly?
- Underline every question in Genesis 3:1-13. How did Satan use his question? What was Satan working toward? How did God use His questions? What was God working toward? How did God's questions bring good and Satan's question bring destruction?
- Read Mark 3:13-19 for the names of Jesus' 12 disciples.

FIND THE MISTAKE

Invite students to compare a mistake-filled copy of the passage with the real thing. As they find mistakes, they notice the truth. Write the

Bible passage word-for-word except for key words. Challenge youth to work in pairs to find the mistakes, one reading the Scripture passage and one circling mistakes in the bogus version. This example from Romans 1:18-25 has the mistakes italicized. Print it without italics.

CIRCLE AND CORRECT EVERY MISTAKE

Find the mistakes by comparing this retelling to Romans 1:18-20:

For the *love* of God is revealed from heaven *toward* all *godliness* and *righteousness* of men, who suppress *lies* in *righteousness,* because that which is known about God is *apparent around them* for God makes it evident to them. For since the creation of *people* His *visible* attributes, His eternal *knowledge* and divine *Son* have been clearly seen, being *misunderstood* through what has been made, so that they are *with* excuse.

FIND THE VERSE

Write facts about a passage on separate cards. Challenge each youth to take a card and find the verse where the fact is found. Repeat until all the facts are taken. This results in repeated reading and better retention of Bible facts.

VARIATION: Write the facts on a worksheet and let students work in pairs to find verses for all the facts. Scramble the order for an added challenge.

FOOTPRINT READING

Write each word of a key verse on a separate footprint and direct youth to read the verses as they step on each footprint.

ADAPTATION: Enlist youth to help you make the footprints. They'll learn as they write and as they watch others read.

ADAPTATION: For long passages, put a phrase on each footprint.

MY NAME IN THE BIBLE

Read the passage with your students' names in place of *you* and other personal pronouns. "For God so loved *Judy* that He gave His only Son." Pupils' ears will prick up and they'll search the passage for the promises and instructions addressed to them.

NAMES ON BACK

To guide youth to read the passage repeatedly, select key words or phrases from your passage, write them on strips of paper, and tape on to the back of each youth. Do not allow any to read the one on his or her own back. Challenge youth to discover their identity by reading the passage and asking "yes" or "no" questions. Insist that all stay standing and circulating until all have discovered their identity.

ORDER THE FACTS
Write or draw phrases from the passage, one to a card. Scramble the cards and challenge students to read the passage so they can put the cards in order. For long passages, write events on the cards.

ADAPTATION: Prepare a set of scrambled cards for every trio of youth. The fewer on a team, the more each member is involved.

VARIATION: Let youth prepare a set of cards for the other team(s). They learn twice: once when writing cards, once when sorting.

VARIATION: Illustrate the events for students to identify as well as order.

OUT-OF-PLACE POSTERS
Display a copy of the key Bible verse on a poster on the floor, on the ceiling, in the doorway, or in some other out-of-the-way place. An unusual location attracts attention and motivates students to read. Increase interest by encoding the passage or presenting it in rebus form.

WALK AND READ
Create Bible reading posters by folding paper in half, writing a question about the passage inside each poster, and posting the posters in order around the room. Challenge youth to find facts about the passage by opening each folded poster and answering the questions inside. Emphasize that the answers are in the Bible passage (write the reference inside each flip poster so youth can remember where to look). Provide paper to write answers and allow youth to work in pairs. Debrief by giving each pair a flip poster and instructing them to read the question and answer.

The following sample guides youth to study 1 Corinthians 15. Do not print the answer, which are in italics.

FLIP POSTER 1: Read 1 Corinthians 15:1-4 for the three main facts of the Gospel. *(1. Christ died for our sins; 2. Christ was buried; 3. Christ was raised on the third day.)*

FLIP POSTER 2. Read 1 Corinthians 15:5-8 to name six people or groups of people Jesus appeared to after His resurrection. *(1. Peter; 2. the Twelve; 3. More than 500 brothers; 4. James; 5. All the disciples; 6. Me/Paul)*

FLIP POSTER 3. Read 1 Corinthians 15:9-11 to discover what Paul called himself. *(The least of the apostles)*

FLIP POSTER 4. Read 1 Corinthians 15:12-13 to discover who has not been raised if there is no Resurrection. *(Jesus Christ)*

FLIP POSTER 5. Read 1 Corinthians 15:14-19 for five sad results if Christ has not been raised. *(1. Our preaching is useless; 2. So is your faith; 3. We are found to be false witnesses; 4. Those who are dead in Christ are lost; 5. We have hope only in this life)*

FLIP POSTER 6. Read 1 Corinthians 15:20-22 to discover in whom we all die and in whom we all can be resurrected. *(Die in Adam; will be made alive in Christ)*

FLIP POSTER 7. Read 1 Corinthians 15:23-28 to find out at least three things that will happen when Jesus comes back. *(Those who belong to Him will be made alive; the end will come; He will put enemies under His feet; God will be all in all)*

WHO AM I?

Discover characteristics and actions of important Bible characters (or things) by using "Who am I?" cards. Write each description and invite each student to take one and determine the character in the Bible passage you provide. This can be especially effective with familiar passages—youth are often surprised to discover something new.

ADAPTATION: Guide youth to write their own "Who am I?" cards and then exchange. Provide a list of people and objects from the passage.

ADAPTATION: Guide youth to write cards about themselves as a get-to-know-you activity or as an expression of their faith.

WORD SEARCH PLUS

As youth arrive, give them a word search puzzle with key words from the day's passage. Instead of referring to a list of words to find, youth must search the passage for key words. This encourages Bible study because youth read the passage repeatedly to complete this assignment.

A basic word search consists of rows of letters, some of which spell words. Create word searches by selecting key words from the passage. Write these on graph paper vertically, horizontally, and diagonally. Write some of the words backwards. Fill in the blank squares with random consonants (no vowels to keep from spelling words accidentally). Duplicate one copy for each student.

To enhance a word search WHILE youth seek the words:

● *Where?* As they find the words in the word search puzzle, direct students to write the verse where the word is used.

● *How many?* Tell youth how many words to find. Encourage them to check off the words in their Bibles as they find them.

● *How long?* Direct youth to race against the clock to find the words.

● *Race:* Divide into pairs and motivate youth to compete against one another. Competition is almost always a good motivator.

To enhance a word search AFTER youth have found the words:

● *Summary sentence:* Instruct youth to summarize the passage in one sentence, using as many of the word search words as they can without repeating the Bible verses themselves.

● *My favorite word:* Invite each youth to choose a word and tell what it teaches about God or the specific Bible concept you're studying.

● *My favorite phrase:* Invite each youth to read a favorite verse or verse portion that uses one of the words and tell why they like it.

PLUS ...

Try these other options for reading your Bible passage:

● Print the passage with no spaces. Students must divide the words correctly, comparing the passage to the Bible to verify.

● Read in unison several times, each time more quickly than before.

● Read responsively.

● Do a "Conversational Reading" with youth pretending to be Bible characters.

● Find what the passage teaches about God's character or expectations.

● Invite students to look for the phrase in an assigned passage that most specifically speaks to their lives at this time.

● Use any Bible learning game in chapter 5 to focus on key passages.

5
Learning Games
Games Can Attract and Focus Attention on the Bible

Rationale: Learning games are not merely entertaining. Games become meaningful ways to learn Bible facts because they attract and keep youth's attention. Almost any game can be adapted for use in youth Bible study by substituting questions about the Bible passage for the questions in the game. When used well, games become meaningful ways to learn because:

● *Success with the Bible in class motivates use of the Bible at home.* Finding answers in their Bibles during a game motivates students to look to the Bible for answers at home.

● *Youth are already interested in games.* Their natural interest focuses their attention on the Bible passage studied during the game.

● *Youth have a natural drive toward competition.* This makes them work hard to win. Use the competition as motivation to pay attention, not as a tool for putting down losers. In the best learning games, every team wins at least one round.

● *Youth want to succeed in front of their peers.* The best games make it probable that this will happen. Remember, success with the Bible, not winning or losing, is the goal of a learning game.

● *Youth want to look smart.* Well-designed learning games give youth opportunity to shine in front of their peers. A game gives youth less "school fear" than a discussion or worksheet. When the answers come directly from the Bible, youth can find them and they gain confidence in their ability to answer and understand Bible questions.

● *Moving encourages attention.* If the body is moving, the brain can't go to sleep. In discussions, one or two people tend to answer all the questions. Learning games invite participation from the entire group.

● *Youth don't realize they're learning.* This offers several advantages: Those who feel uncertain about their ability to learn relax and learn more effectively; those who might not succeed in a classroom setting often succeed at learning games and thus trust their ability to understand the Bible. Even the wisest Bible students usually learn something new during a learning game.

Learning games can be used with any Bible passage but are best when the passage contains plenty of detail. Use the questions in your printed curriculum for game questions or make up your own, taking them directly from the Bible passage.

Teaching Tip: Encourage youth to keep their Bibles open at all times during learning games. If they don't bring their own Bible, give them one. The goal of learning games is success with the Bible.

Teaching Tip: Make an answer key for yourself. Write the question, followed by the verse reference and answer. In the excitement of leading the game you may find it hard to recall answers.

Teaching Tip: To avoid complaints of favoritism in the distribution of questions, let players draw questions from a bag, or number the questions and have players request a question by number without seeing the list.

Teaching Tip: Avoid Bible games that pull the questions from the entire Bible or from several passages at once. Even the best Bible students have difficulty succeeding at these. Focus on one or two passages so players can learn the passage(s) thoroughly. Remember: Bible learning, not game expertise, is the goal of Bible learning games.

BIBLE CONCENTRATION

The goal of memory or concentration games is to turn over identical cards from a set of numbered cards. Adapt this to Bible learning by matching pairs that complete one another. Types of completions:

● Half a Bible phrase on one card and half on the other card;
● A Bible term on one card and a definition on the other;
● A person on one and a description of the person on the other;
● A person on one and an action or quote by that person on the other.

A study of the last week of Jesus' life might use the following matches:

PETER   Said he would never deny Jesus but denied Him three times (Mark 14:72)

SOLDIERS   Put a purple robe on Jesus to mock Him (Mark 15:16-20)

PROCESS OF PLAY

1. Create the game by writing cards that complete one another. Write each part on a separate card. Write the verse references on the second card of each pair so players can verify the matches in their Bibles. Prepare set of game cards for every two to six youth.

2. Shuffle each set of cards and arrange face-down in rows. Challenge players to take turns making matches. Direct them to check their answers in their Bibles.

RULES

1. Turn over two cards at a time. If they match, keep them. If not, turn them back over. Verify your matches with the Bible references.

2. If you make a correct match, it is still the other player's turn. This gives everyone an equal chance.

FOLLOW-UP

Invite students to tell about the cards they matched, using their Bibles or student book for commentary. Supplement from your teacher's book or commentary.

ADAPTATIONS

• Enlist an artistic youth to draw a rebus to place under the concentration game. A rebus is a combination of words and pictures that states the theme or focal verse of your Bible study (see chapter 12). Challenge players to solve the rebus as they make matches.

• Let students make concentration games for each other. They learn twice: once creating the game and once playing.

BIBLE JEOPARDY

In this Bible learning game, you give the answers and your students ask the questions. It works well with a detailed passage, when studying a large amount of text, or when reviewing several sessions.

PROCESS OF PLAY

1. Write questions that come directly from your passage(s). Trans-

late these questions into answers and make an answer key. (Writing your questions first keeps the answers from answering several questions.) If, while studying Genesis 9, you want your youth to know, "What blessing did God give Noah and his sons?" your answer becomes, "The blessing God gave Noah and his sons," not, "The blessing." Note these other examples:

What could Noah eat that he could not eat before?	*becomes*	What Noah could eat that he could not eat before (9:3).	*and the question is:* "What is meat?"
What does the rainbow stand for?	*becomes*	The meaning of the rainbow (9:13).	*and the question is:* "What is the sign of God's covenant to never flood the earth again?"

2. Arrange your "answers" according to category. You might have one category for each session of a five-session study, one for each section of a student book, or one for each theme.

3. Arrange the answers in order of difficulty, the easiest worth 10 points and the hardest worth 50 points.

4. Set the game up one of these ways:

a. Write each answer on a page and cover it with a page declaring its point value. Tape these to the wall in rows by category. Lift the top sheet to reveal the answer.

b. Write each answer on paper and place it in an envelope marked with the point value. Open the envelope to reveal the answer.

c. Write the answers on a single piece of white paper in rows. Make an overhead transparency of this paper. Tape a square over each answer. Project the "board" on the wall. Lift the papers to reveal answers.

5. Play by the rules that follow.

RULES

1. The person with the birthday closest to today chooses the first category and point value, then reads the answer.

2. The first person to stand gives the question to the answer. Because you lose points for incorrect questions, think and consult with your team before standing. Because you are racing against others, stand as soon as you think you know.

3. Whoever comes up with the correct question chooses the next category and point value.

4. Correct questioners earn the points for that answer. Incorrect questioners lose the points for that answer.

5. Keep your Bibles open to the passage at all times. To be correct, you must name the verse where you got the answer.

FOLLOW-UP

Comment on Bible facts as they come up in the game. Point out how your students learned by reviewing the facts when the game is ended.

ADAPTATIONS

● If your group is small, challenge them to play individually. If your group is large, play in teams, encouraging teams to consult before giving answers. See appendix B for suggestions for dividing into teams.

● Let students create their own answers week by week. Use for review.

BIBLE TRIVIA

In this adaptation of the trivia board game, questions come from the Bible passage you are studying. Correct answers are rewarded with triangles in six colors. The first team to collect all six triangles wins. As with all learning games, write your questions directly from Scripture and instruct your students to keep their Bibles open and take their answers directly from Scripture.

PROCESS OF PLAY

1. Use a die covered with six colors or make your own by covering a standard die with six construction paper squares.

2. Cut out six triangles for each team from the six colors on your die.

3. Divide youth into teams of about four. Seat the teams opposite each other: two teams in two rows, three teams in a triangle, four teams in a square, five teams in a pentagon, and so on.

4. Explain and play by the rules that follow.

RULES

1. The first team draws a question and confers before answering.

Be certain answers come directly from the Bible passage and are not just guesses.

2. If your answer is correct, roll the die and receive a triangle in that color. Display the triangles on the floor in front of your team. If your team rolls a color it already has, you win no triangle.

3. Teams take turns until one team has six triangles.

4. Every team member must answer a question (after conferring with the team) before any team member may take a second turn.

FOLLOW-UP

Comment on questions as they are answered. After the game, quiz youth briefly to demonstrate how much they have learned about the passage.

ADAPTATIONS

• Use the game to study text from your student book or theme materials. It works well with large bodies of material.

• Prepare the questions in categories and let players roll the die to choose a category. If correct, they win a triangle in that color.

• Make your entire room into a game board by laying down squares of construction paper in the colors of the categories. The first player rolls a die, walks that number of spaces (starting anywhere), and confers with his or her teammates to answer a question. The player stays on that square while the opposing team takes a turn, when he is replaced by the next person on his team. Each team gets only one question per turn, and wins a triangle for each correct answer. The first team to collect triangles in all the colors wins.

• Play like the board game using only certain squares as award squares. This version is more time-consuming.

FACT MATCH

Write the first half of a Bible fact on one card and the second half on a second card. Shuffle all the cards and challenge youth to match them correctly. Encourage them to keep their eyes on their Bible passage as they match.

PROCESS OF PLAY

• **Human match:** Give each youth a card and challenge them to find the person who matches. They verify their matches in the Bible.

• **Match race:** Make two sets of cards and give them to two teams. Challenge each team to race to match the cards before the other team.

● **Match in my hand:** Hold the first half of each match in your hand. Display the second halves randomly on the floor or table. Hold one up and challenge youth to find its match. Or let youth draw an unseen card from your hand and match it to those on the floor or table.

RULES

1. You must keep your Bible open to the passage being studied to verify matches. Resist the temptation to guess because you'll learn nothing new.

2. Teams may work together and encourage each other.

FOLLOW-UP

Guide youth to find facts in their student books about the match they made. Invite them to report.

Challenge youth to recite the matches (or parts of the matches) from memory to show how much they learned during the game.

ADAPTATIONS

● Each time a match is made, invite youth to tell why that fact is important to the Bible event, how it influences their life, or what they like about it.

● Guide youth to make matching games for each other.

GUESS THE WORD

This adaption of the game "Password" is quick to prepare and easy to use. It results in memorizing a series of Bible words or themes.

Playing with key words from a single passage motivates students to read the passage repeatedly and thus better understand and remember it. Playing with theme is harder because students must depend on several passages at once, but it helps pull together a major Bible theme. Post the verses to make the game less frustrating.

PROCESS OF PLAY

1. Choose one passage and select the key words from it. Passwords from 1 Timothy 4:12 include: YOUNG, EXAMPLE, BELIEVERS, SPEECH, LIFE, LOVE, FAITH, PURITY.

If you play the theme version, choose a theme such as names for

God, characters in the Christmas event or other Bible events, books of the Bible, etc. Using a topical Bible, find passages that tell about your theme.

2. Prepare a set of password cards by writing each word on a separate card. Thick cards keep players from reading through.

3. Prepare one set of cards for every five students expected. Four will play the game while one serves as cluegiver/scorekeeper.

4. Set up four chairs for each game:

B b

D d

Partners face each other and sit next to their opponents. In the above illustration, the B's are partners and the D's are partners.

5. The cluegiver/scorekeeper (you, if your class is small) shows the first password to one side (capital letters in the illustration). B gives a one-word clue to his partner, b, who is allowed to search the passage before answering.

6. If b answers correctly, the B's earn 10 points. If not, D gives a one-word clue to d. If d is correct, the D's get 9 points.

7. Alternate cluegiving until one is correct or point value is 0.

8. Then next round, show the password to the other side (lower-case letters in illustration). Let d give the first clue so the D's have a chance to make 10 points. Alternate until all words are guessed or time expires.

RULES

1. Your job is to work with your partner to guess the passwords.

2. When you give a clue, use only one word and no part of the password. Use no gestures.

3. First guesses are final, even if a mistake. Look in your Bible for the answer before speaking.

FOLLOW-UP

While playing, briefly discuss each word as it is guessed. If you are studying names of Christ you might ask, "How is Jesus like a door in your life?"

After the game, discuss in more detail questions that show how the words relate to each other. If you are using names of Christ ask, "Which name for Jesus is your favorite? How does it affect the way you relate to Him?"

Invite volunteers to make a single sentence using all the passwords.

ADAPTATIONS

• This game can get confusing if players have several Bible translations. Accept as correct the answer that comes from the translation in the youth's lap. For example, "conduct" in the New American Standard Version means the same as "life" in the New International Version.

• Let students make password cards for other teams. They'll learn as they make the game and again as they play.

• If you have six students, play with three teams instead of two.

• If adults are available, let them serve as cluegivers/scorekeepers.

HUMAN TIC-TAC-TOE

To review units of study or to study details in a specific passage, play Bible tic-tac-toe. It is a great fact-discovery procedure.

PROCESS OF PLAY

1. Arrange the chairs in three rows of three chairs, like a tic-tac-toe board. Arrange remaining chairs in two groups, one group on each side of the human size board.

X	h h h	O
players	h h h	players
here	h h h	here

2. Get questions from your curriculum or by writing them yourself. You'll need at least nine questions for each round of play.

3. Divide your group into two teams. (See appendix B for suggestions.) Seat teams on opposite sides of the tic-tac-toe "board." Give one team paper X's and the other team O's. Provide masking tape to attach the letters and insist that all players wear them.

4. Challenge each team to seat three correct answers in a row. Explain that the game is "open-book": all answers come directly from the Bible passage. Post the Bible verses for easy reference.

5. Explain and play by the rules that follow.

RULES

1. X team goes first. An X brings his Bible to the tic-tac-toe board and sits in the chair his team chooses.

2. The team member must answer with no help from his team but with lots of help from his Bible. If correct, X stays in the chair. If not, he returns to his seat.

3. The O's must pay close attention while X is in the chair. If X misses, O's may consult among themselves and send a member to answer that same question. If O misses, the X's may consult and send a member to answer the same question.

4. No team member may play a second time before all play once.

5. The first team to seat three players in a row wins.

FOLLOW-UP

During and following the game, highlight points about the Bible passage on which the game is based. Let commentary flow naturally from the game process. For example, when you ask "What did God say about Jesus when He was baptized?" and a player answers, "This is my Son, whom I love; with Him I am well pleased," explain that these words show that Jesus is God's Son and that Jesus' baptism marked the beginning of His ministry.

Following the game, point out to your students' that during this game they studied the Bible. Ask a few questions from the game to demonstrate what they've learned.

ADAPTATIONS

● If your room is too small to set up three rows of chairs, mark off a tic-tac-toe board with masking tape on the floor. Players stand on the squares.

● If your room is too small for floor squares, display a tic-tac-toe board on the table or wall and let players place their X's and O's.

● This game is best with groups of 10 to 20 youth but can be played with as few as 2. With huge groups, divide into groups and play multiple games. With smaller groups, students leave the paper X or O in the chair.

● Consider a 30-second time limit, but remember that learning, not speed, is your goal.

● If someone misses, state that she had an especially hard question. Teens find it easier to accept missing a hard question.

LETTER BOARD

Popularized as "Boggle," this game challenges students to circle all the words they can find in a block of letters. Create the letter board with four or five key phrases from the Bible passage. Circling even unrelated words keeps players reading the Bible passage or passage portion. A letter board works well as an arrival activity because early arrivers get the most words and so receive positive attention for arriving on time.

PROCESS OF PLAY

1. Create the game by underlining or writing key phrases.

2. Type your phrases one to a line with one space between each letter, word, and line. Add these directions at the top:

Circle all the words you can find in this block of letters. Words can be vertical, horizontal, diagonal, backward, or forward. You can count plural words twice (once in singular, once in plural) and words within words (example: JESUS also contains US).

A sample quote letter board for Isaiah 9:6:

```
W  O  N  D  E  R  F  U  L  C  O  U  N  S  E  L  O  R
M  I  G  H  T  Y  G  O  D
E  V  E  R  L  A  S  T  I  N  G  F  A  T  H  E  R
P  R  I  N  C  E  O  F  P  E  A  C  E
```

3. Duplicate the letter boards, one for every pair of students. Explain and play by the following rules.

RULES

1. Your job is to circle and write all words with your partner.
2. Words you circle must be authentic. Proper names count.

FOLLOW-UP

Challenge volunteers to repeat the phrases without looking. The game process will have helped them memorize at least part of the phrases.

Because players will complain if you don't score, call for each pair to count their words. Award the winning one with generous applause.

ADAPTATIONS

● Use phrases that relate to your theme, as in the sample that follows.

● Guide students to create a letter board by writing the main truth of the lesson each week. The truths become a review letter board.

● Allow words made of any adjacent letters, even if the letters are not in a straight line. For example: *tailor* and *hives* in the sample below.

```
F O R G I V E N E S S H E A L S
R E L A T I O N S H I P S
B E I N G F O R G I V E N M A K E S
F O R G I V I N G E A S I E R
W O N D E R F U L C O U N S E L O R
M I G H T Y G O D
E V E R L A S T I N G F A T H E R
P R I N C E O F P E A C E
```

PENCIL CHARADES

Popularized as "Win, Lose, or Draw" and "Pictionary," this game works well as the "read the Bible passage" portion of the Bible study. Your students will be reading the passage with intensity.

PROCESS OF PLAY

1. Underline key phrases in the passage. Pay little attention to how easy the phrase is to draw. Youth have amazing ability and will be watching the passage for clues.

2. Write each key phrase on a card. Bring a pad and marker or chalkboard and chalk.

3. Bring blank cards for scorekeeping. Plan to give teams a card for each 100 points they earn. The team with the most cards wins.

4. Divide into teams of about five.

5. Explain and play by the rules that follow.

RULES

1. The person with the birthday closest to today goes first. This artist views a card and draws the phrase for the team on a chalkboard or large pad. Use drawings only, no numbers or words.

2. The phrase comes directly from Isaiah 53 (or whatever passage you're studying) so keep your Bibles open while you guess.

3. Once a word is guessed, the artist can write that word above the drawing.

4. If the whole phrase is guessed within one minute, your team earns 200 points. If it is guessed within two minutes, your team earns 100 points.

5. There are no penalties for mistaken guesses.

FOLLOW-UP

After each correct guess, comment on the Bible phrase. After the game, ask a few fact questions about the passage to demonstrate how much contestants have learned.

ADAPTATIONS

● Rather than having one team drawing at a time, let teams race: Call an artist from each team. Show the artists the same phrase. On "GO" they return to their teams and draw on paper on the floor. The first team to shout the correct answer wins points.

● Weekly ask your students to underline the three phrases they think are most important in the passage. Then review the unit of study (at the end of that session or the beginning of the next) with pencil charades. List the passages so students can leaf back and forth to them, but don't say which phrase came from which passage.

● Act out charades instead of drawing.

● Draw Bible attitudes, both good and bad.

ROOM-SIZED BIBLE STUDY GAMES

Room-sized games are simply enlargements of board or TV games. Keep the process of play and rules but take the questions from the Bible.

A room-sized game can be as quick to make as laying out several pieces of paper in a road. It can be as complex as creating an adaptation of a television game show complete with emcee and fancy spinner. Consider these possibilities:

● **Generic game:** Lay out several pieces of paper with questions written on the back of each piece. Players roll a die, walk the number of pieces, pick up the paper, and answer the question using their Bibles. Once a piece is answered, turn it face up. When someone lands on a face-up page, she may ask a Bible question or choose the piece before or after that one.

● **Newly Christian game:** Create three or four questions on the theme of the passage. For example, for Galatians 6:1-5 you might choose:

1. Tell a burden you bore for your friend.
2. Tell about a burden your friend bore for you.
3. Tell about a Christian action your partner can be proud of.

Enlist two to eight confident pairs of youth to play the "Newly Christian Game." Partners should know each other fairly well. Give each player three cards and direct them to write the answers to the questions you give, without letting their partners see their answers. With their answer cards face down in their laps, ask one member of each pair to answer the first question the way he thinks his partner answered. Direct the partner to hold up the answer she wrote. Continue for the other questions, alternating the partner who goes first. Follow up with an open discussion of the passage.

SCRIPTURE BASEBALL
Scripture baseball is played with a diamond of four chairs.

PROCESS OF PLAY
1. Arrange four chairs as bases of a baseball diamond. Arrange remaining chairs in two groups, one on each side of the diamond.

2. Get questions from your curriculum or write them yourself. Number the questions and write the verse reference and answer after each. Divide questions into singles, doubles, or triples according to difficulty. Or singles can have one answer, doubles two, and triples three answers. Older youth tend to choose triples because if they miss they can say the question was too hard. Younger youth choose more singles, hoping to answer correctly. Write more of what your group likes.

3. Divide your group into two teams (see appendix B for suggestions). Seat teams on opposite sides of the baseball diamond.

4. Challenge each team to bat in as many runners as possible by answering Bible questions. Explain they can do this with singles, doubles, or triples.

5. Explain that the game is "open-book": all answers come directly from the Bible passage. Post the Bible references.

6. Explain and play by the rules that follow until all questions are asked or time is up.

RULES
1. The batter with the birthday closest to today goes first. The batter chooses a question (single, double, or triple) and sits in that chair with his Bible.

2. The team member must answer with no help from his team but with lots of help from his Bible. If he is correct, he stays in that chair.

If not, he is out and the other team is up. (One out per inning keeps sides changing.)

3. The opposing team must pay close attention while a batter is in the chair. If the batter misses, the opposing team may consult among themselves and send a batter to answer that same question. (This rule helps both teams pay attention and to look up all answers.)

4. All batters ahead of a new batter advance as many chairs as the new batter. If one batter is on second and the new batter chooses a double, the second-base batter moves to home.

5. No team member may play a second time before all play once.

6. The decision of the judge will be final.

7. Encouraging words may be rewarded with extra points.

FOLLOW-UP

As questions are answered, highlight points about the Bible passage. Let discussion flow naturally from the game.

Challenge students to reread the passage for a truth they are glad they know. Call for several to share why this truth is meaningful to them.

ADAPTATIONS

• The one disadvantage to Scripture baseball is that someone has to miss for the other team to get a turn. Be certain to bolster the confidence of those who miss by talking about how hard the question was. Rather than having players draw questions at random, choose the questions yourself, gearing them to the student's ability. Self-esteem takes priority over randomness.

• Consider a 30-second time limit. This allows you to bolster those who miss with, "If you'd just had more time, you would have gotten it."

• If your room is too small for the chairs, mark a baseball diamond with masking tape on the table, floor, or wall and let players make paper images of themselves to run around the diamond.

• Get your questions from curriculum or the Bible passage.

TRADING GAME

Popularized as "Pit," the trading game guides youth to memorize Bible passages or to preview or review important concepts. Beginning with a set of cards that do not match, players trade to collect identical cards. Repeatedly seeing the cards as they trade helps youth memorize the items that pass through their hands. Create a trading game with any list from the Bible. Possibilities include: fruit of the Spirit (Galatians 5:22-23); characteristics of love (1 Corinthians 13:4-7); spiritual gifts (Romans 12:6-8; Ephesians 4:11-13; 1 Corinthians 12:7-11); the Ten Commandments (Exodus 20).

PROCESS OF PLAY
1. List the actions, words, or characteristics you want to study.
2. Write each on four cards. Four cards form a matching set.
3. Create a set of four cards for each player. Duplicate sets if you have more students than words. Play twice if you have fewer students than words.
4. Shuffle the cards and distribute so youth have four non-matching cards.
5. Explain the rules and play by the rules that follow.

RULES
1. You have four non-matching cards. Each is a fruit of the Spirit (or whatever your theme). When I say go, obtain a set of four matching cards by trading one or more cards at a time. Don't show the cards you trade.
2. You may find that someone else is trying to save what you are trying to save. Feel free to change to saving something else.
3. When you finish, find your characteristic in the Bible passage (or student book) and prepare to tell how to use it.

FOLLOW-UP
Call on all players to name their fruit of the Spirit (or other theme) and tell how it would bring about good at their schools.

Invite volunteers to name all the nine fruits (or other theme).

ADAPTATIONS
● Play "Spoons" with a shuffled deck of trading cards. Youth pass cards around the circle, keeping only four at a time. The first to collect four of a kind picks up a spoon from the center of the circle.

● Give matching cards initially and instruct youth to trade until they have one of each different card.

● The trading game also works well with theme studies. Sample: Four types of prayer: PRAISE, PETITION, CONFESSION, INTERCESSION.

PLUS...

These games have been successfully adapted for Bible study. How might you use these or something similar?

- Bible bowl (like College Bowl quiz games with buzzers and teams);
  - Slapjack (slap cards that agree with the Bible passage);
  - Bible football (downs for correct answers);
  - Simulate a Bible problem and solve it for points;
  - Relay race (run up, answer the question correctly, run back);
  - Wheel of Fortune (a version of hangman; see chapter 7);
  - Family Feud;
  - Ungame, Sorry, Monopoly, and other board games;
  - What's My Line?
  - Fruit Basket Turnover;
  - Twenty Questions;
  - Jigsaw puzzles (good for studying the body of Christ or for assembling a portion of Scripture);
  - Fake money (use in a study of stewardship).

6
Creative Questioning

Good Questions Motivate Students to Search the Bible,
Not Guess What's in Your Head

Rationale: Questions help make the transition from fact to understanding. But simply quizzing students can turn them off, put them on the defensive, and make them clam up. This chapter provides a variety of question formats you can use to keep students interested and involved.

Teaching Tip: Reduce student anxiety over giving wrong answers by taking initial questions directly from the Bible passage and gently moving forward to application questions. Success with God's Word, not ranking kids in answering ability, is our goal.

Bonus Section: How to Ask Good Questions: These ASKING tips help lead to solid Bible learning:

Apply the Bible to life. Keep in mind your ultimate goal of God's Word changing lives. Let each question move toward this goal by helping youth understand a Bible verse or helping them see how that verse translates into action.

Simple to complex. Begin with fact questions and proceed to interpretation questions. Move from "who?" and "what?" to "how?" and "why?"

Keep the answer source apparent. Make sure students know where to look for answers. Usually this source is the Bible itself; other times it is commentary about the Bible; occasionally it is youth's own experience. Post the reference to keep the forgetful on track.

Involve every youth. Use question methods that encourage all youth to respond, not just the most confident or vocal. "Under-Chair Questions," "Talk Around the Circle," and similar processes get all youth involved in the learning. Teacher-asking-and-students-responding-at-random involves the fewest youth.

Never answer your own question. Internally count to 20 before speaking, remembering that you've been thinking about the question since you prepared, but your students have just heard it. If they still struggle, repeat the question in a different way or clarify the answer source: "Look in John 3 for. . . ."

Grab interest by varying your words. Rather than limiting yourself to who, what, when, where, why, and how, consider these possibilities: Adapt, apply, approximate, arrange, categorize, choose, circle, star, underline, compare, compose, count, define, demonstrate, discover, diagnose, estimate, evaluate, expand upon, explain, figure out, identify, illustrate, imagine, investigate, list, organize, perfect, plan, ponder, quote, recognize, relate, respond, show, skim, sketch, solve, suggest, theorize, translate.

ANSWER OPTIONS

Some youth are comfortable with words. Others, equally as smart, would rather draw or doodle or dramatize their answer. Still others want to give an example. Offer several ways to respond to your question to enable all these students to learn.

ATTITUDE TO ACTION

Guide youth beyond "churchy" answers to specific ones. When they answer, "Be loving" ask, "How would you show you are a loving person?" Other questions to encourage demonstration of Christian attitudes include "What words would you use to show forgiveness?" "What action would demonstrate your compassion?" "What facial expression shows patience?"

BRAINSTORM

To brainstorm is to list rapidly every answer that comes to mind and refrain from evaluating them until all are down. Because all participants shout answers at the same time, youth feel a little more comfortable joining in. Brainstorming is also valuable because it generates many solutions to a problem or answers to a question. It makes the best solution easier to find.

To make brainstorming effective, accept and write down all answers, even those you know to be off-the-wall. This helps youth to know you are listening and gives them courage to say more honest answers.

To make brainstorming valuable, be certain to evaluate the final list with questions like these: Which of these are most likely to work and why? Which are least likely to work and why? Which are right according to the Bible? Which are wrong according to the Bible?

CREATE QUIZZES

Challenge pairs of youth to create quizzes with five questions based on the passage you are studying. Assign each pair to a different passage or section of the Bible commentary. Agree on a format for quizzes, such as true/false, multiple choice, fill-in-the-blank, one-word answer, multi-word answer, matching, mazes (see chapter 11).

HOT BAG

Any time your curriculum includes a series of questions, cut them apart, place them in a small paper sack, and play "hot bag." Twist the top of the sack and pass it around your circle like a "hot potato." Direct players to pass the bag until the music stops. With your back turned, play music or hum "Jesus Loves Me." When the music stops, the one holding the bag draws out a question and answers it. Encourage students to keep their Bibles open in their laps to find the answer quickly.

This simple prop adds great motivation for finding Bible answers. It is also valuable for sharing solutions to problems in the bag. Control pandemonium with rules like "pass the bag at a steady pace" and "pass to the person next to you rather than across the circle."

I WAS THERE

Direct students to answer questions from the point of view of one of the characters in the passage you are studying. Call on them to say what they see, feel, hear, and think (perhaps also smell and taste in some passages).

VARIATION: Guide youth to doodle, draw, or write their experiences.

VARIATION: Provide name tags to help youth recall who is who.

VARIATION: Use this with theme studies also. During a study on witnessing, one youth can be skeptical, one rebellious, one open.

LET STUDENTS ASK THE QUESTIONS

A successful way to involve youth is to let them do the teaching. Give one student your questions (with the answer key) and invite him or her to ask the class the questions. Alternate "teachers" every few questions.

LIFE QUESTIONS

Make your questions as related to life as possible. Listen to what your students talk about before and after class and gear your questions to these issues. Some classics include:

• How does this verse impact how we relate to our parents? How we'd like them to relate to us?

• Tell about a mistake you made. How can this verse help fix it?

• What was the hardest decision you ever made?

• How do you know God is real?

• What worries you?

• When have you had this problem? What did you do about it?

• Who is your best friend? How have you stayed close?

• What do you do when your friend lets you down?

• If you could change one thing about your life, what would you change? What do you like about your life?

POINT TO THE ANSWER

As you ask questions about Bible facts, instruct youth to keep their Bibles open. Explain that to be correct, the one answering the question must put her finger on the word or phrase that confirms her answer. This motivates students to search their Bibles rather than just guess.

RIDDLES

Create, or guide youth to create and exchange, riddles that have their answers in the Bible passage you are studying. If you're extra creative, come up with rhyming riddles. Examples for the Tower of Babel (Genesis 11:1-9):

1. Thought it would make a name;
   Seemed obsessed with fame;
   God saw the danger in this power
   And took away this tower.
2. What planned to reach the heavens but heaven reached down to it?

SCAVENGER HUNT

Give each team a list of things to find in a Bible passage. This is especially helpful for long passages or when studying an entire book of the Bible. Pairs work especially well with this type of assignment;

larger groups tend to let one or two do all the work. To make the hunt more challenging, do not give verse or chapter numbers. If you want the activity to go quickly, keep the items in the order they appear in the text.

STAND WHEN YOU KNOW

Divide your group into three or more teams. Direct each team to write five questions based on the passage you assign. Emphasize that the answers must be in the Bible passage.

When questions are written, seat teams across from each other (a triangle of three teams, square of four teams, and so on). Call for a team to read one of its questions. The first member of an opposing team to stand and answer the question wins a point for his or her team. Continue for the other teams. If any team presents a question which no other team can answer in 60 seconds, the team wins 5 points. If one team dominates the answering, introduce a rule that no one team may answer two questions in a row.

This game works well when the teams write questions on the same passage. This way youth get double learning: when writing the questions and when answering them. The game also works well by dividing a long passage. Players then answer by searching that section of the Bible passage.

ADAPTATION: Write the questions yourself prior to the session.

TALK AROUND THE CIRCLE

Invite participation with a rule that everyone around the circle must add something to the discussion in turn. If anyone can't think of an answer in 15 seconds, he or she stands up until the next round. This method is effective with both fact-finding and Bible application. It has several inviting variations:

● **Alphabetical answers:** Each answer must begin with a successive letter of the alphabet. If your assignment is characteristics of Jesus and how to live them answers might include: Jesus was Approachable (and I can be approachable by . . .), Bold, Caring. . . .

● **Group story:** Each youth adds another detail to a story. For example, "Chris Christian went to school planning to fight temptation. . . ." Each student adds an episode.

● **Answer by name:** Each gives an answer beginning with the first letter of his name. "I'm Ursula and I resist temptation by Understanding the deception."

• **Answer by verse:** Each must add another detail from the passage. If you are listing characteristics of love from 1 Corinthians 13, each youth adds another characteristic to the list and tells how to live it.

• **Answer repeat:** Remember each person's suggestions by directing students to repeat, in order, all of the previous answers.

• **Alternate answers:** Each suggests "____ instead of ____," starting with the same letter (Act instead of Argue; Walk instead of Worry).

TAPE-RECORDED QUESTIONS

Enlist a person other than yourself to tape-record the questions for that day's passage. Ask that the questioner leave a few seconds of silence between questions. During the sessions, direct youth to pass the recorder, play one question, answer it from the Bible, and pass it to the next youth. The novelty of the tape recorder often maintains youth's attention and interest. Other times they get carried away trying to decide who is talking. If this happens, spend a few moments guessing until the identity of the speaker is confirmed and then move on.

UNDER-CHAIR QUESTIONS

Any time you have a series of questions to answer, tape one under each chair before youth arrive. Challenge kids to remove the question from under their chair and find the answer in the Bible passage. This method encourages everyone to talk and prevents any one from dominating.

ADAPTATION: Save writing time by cutting the questions out of your teacher's book. If you prefer keeping your book intact, duplicate the page and cut apart the duplicated page.

WALK AND FIND

Create a treasure hunt for facts from the Bible passage. Post questions around the room, with each question giving the location of the next question. (For example, "Write four characteristics of the Word [1 John 1:1]. *Look for your next question under the window.")* Let students start at different points in the room for crowd control.

PLUS . . .

Consider these options for investigating a Bible passage:

• Privately complete a challenge found in a sealed envelope (fre-

quently used for personal devotions at retreats).
- Create a family tree for Jesus or an Old Testament character.
- Evaluate a film or filmstrip evaluation.
- Give a headline or title to the Bible passage.
- Use a question box for anonymous questions or for suggestions.
- Pretend to be a psychiatrist or counselor. Give advice to the Bible character.
- Play "Bible Jeopardy" (see chapter 5) or simply use the format of giving answers to elicit questions without introducing points and competition.

7
Writing, Word Puzzles, and More
Use Both Words and Drawings to Express Bible Understanding

Rationale: Putting ideas on paper helps students solidify vague ideas and express thoughts they hesitate to say out loud. Those who feel more comfortable writing thoughts than saying them may feel freer to share once they have written and thought through their ideas.

Make this Bible learning method even more appealing by adding drawing as an option. Cultivate the habit of offering two choices with every assignment: "draw or write," "jot down or doodle," "put into words or illustrate." Drawings can communicate Bible truth as well as words. Both demonstrate understanding of the Bible passage.

Teaching Tip: Let students know, before they write or draw, whether or not they will share what they write. This lets them decide the type of response to write. Private response encourages honest sharing between the student and God but can keep some students from working as hard. Shared response helps all grow from other's insights but may keep some from writing honestly. Consider the happy medium of anonymous response or sharing some, but not all, of what is written.

Bonus Section: Making the Most of Paper: Paper-and-pencil assignments suffer from "school transfer": the dread of repeating the same old assignments or the fear of failing at school-like tasks. Youth get so tired of worksheets and written homework that they resist it anywhere but school (and sometimes at school!). Simply varying the shape, texture, or size of your paper can minimize resistance. The more unusual your paper and the more interesting your assignment, the more youth will pay attention to and learn from it. Avoid standard white 8½ x 11 paper. Instead use papers that are:

- Colored
- Round
- Tiny
- Bookmarks
- Bumper stickers
- Strips
- Bumpy
- Short and fat
- Business cards
- Cut in shapes
- Stick-on notes
- Textured
- Recycled
- Oversized
- Stapled like books

At times use no paper at all: Write on clay to simulate clay tablets. Find huge leaves to approximate papyrus. Write on light bulbs with glass markers. Write Bible principles on hands as though preparing "cheat" notes for the tests of life.

Take advantage of ways youth already write: phone numbers, notes to pass, diary entries, T-shirts, and more. To make the writing meaningful, always relate it both to the Bible passage and to real life. Use questions like: How has this writing or drawing made the Bible's truth more clear? How has it shown how you can live the Bible at school? How does it invite friends to become interested in living Christ's way?

ACROSTIC

An acrostic uses the letters of the alphabet or a word to recall characteristics of that word or theme. Psalm 119 is an acrostic of the Hebrew alphabet, each section beginning with the next letter of the alphabet. Readers remember the points by going through the alphabet or the acrostic word.

Rather than just writing the acrostic on a poster, cut letters from half sheets of paper and give each youth one. They then write on the letter and assemble them in words.

Consider these possibilities:

- Search John 1 for characteristics of Jesus that start with each letter of His name. Sample:

> John told about Him
> Existed in the beginning
> Sent from the Father
> Unrecognized by the world but received by those who believed in His name
> Shows us God

- Write your first name vertically on paper. Beginning with each letter of your name, state ways you can show you are a Christian. Refer to James 1:19-27 for ideas.
- Use a passage like Philippians 2 to find ideas for an acrostic of the word *humility.*

ADVICE LETTERS

Guide youth to write "Dear Abby" letters asking advice for current problems related to the topic you're studying. Then shuffle the letters, redistribute, and let students write advice. The advice-giver reads the problem and his advice and then asks the group for other ideas. Youth love to get one another's advice, so this process tends to be instantly successful.

VARIATION: Challenge youth to pretend they are Satan and write a letter tempting a specific temptation. Exchange and give suggestions about resisting the temptation.

BUTTONS

Make buttons from circles of poster board or sticky paper. Give each student a circle, a marker, and an assignment to summarize the truths of the passage. For example:

• If Jesus (or another Bible person) wore a button, what would it say?

• What does this passage make you want to do?

• What does this passage make you want to be like?

• Create a coded message that summarizes this passage.

Invite kids to wear the buttons to church, attach them to their Bibles, put them on their coat, or post them at home.

VARIATION: Rings or armbands serve the same purpose.

CHARTS

Charts can make complex truths clear or show divisions between right and wrong, helpful and destructive, Christian and non-Christian. Possibilities for group charts include:

• Qualities of the old life vs. qualities of the new life;

• Reactions of the thief on the left and the thief on the right of Jesus;

• Events that happened during each time in Bible history (similar to a time line except youth write on it);

• Chart the love/ministry/growth of our group.

Possibilities for individual charts include:

• Chart your spiritual growth, labeling ups and downs.

• Chart your week, labeling times you lived for Christ and times you ignored Him.

• Write what you want to be doing in 10 years on the right side of your paper. Then add, in order, the steps to get there.

Interesting formats for charts include:

- Flip charts (students open them to find question or statement inside);
- Strip charts (open one strip at a time);
- Words that wind, go upside down, or otherwise invite you to follow;
- Banners (long with large letters to focus on the theme);
- Cling charts (like flannel boards—add and remove items);
- Column charts (each column adds to the previous);
- Ceiling posters, door/floor/on-person posters;
- Put-together posters (involves youth as they assemble).

ADAPTATION: Youth may get bored with a chart if only one or two people can write on it at a time. Solve this by laying the chart across the table or floor and giving everyone a marker or by cutting the chart apart and guiding teams to work in categories.

CROSSWORD GRID

A crossword grid is a crossword puzzle without definition clues. As in a crossword puzzle, the words must share letters and youth must work from the same Bible translation. Unlike the crossword puzzle, no clues are needed because the words are all drawn from the Bible verse. Youth place every word or key word of the verse or verses into the grid. Fitting the words to the grid encourages youth to read the verse repeatedly.

To prepare a crossword grid:

1. Write the words of the verse in order from longest to shortest.

2. Arrange the words on graph paper so each crosses with another, beginning with the longest word. If words don't fit, skip them and come back when you see opportunity

3. Mark off the grid with no letters filled in.

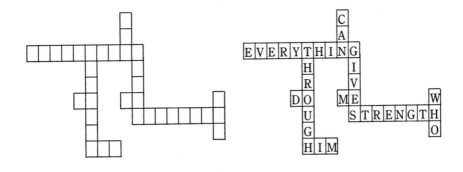

CROSSWORD PUZZLE

This familiar activity appeals to youth because they know how to do it. The best Bible crossword puzzles draw their words and clues directly from the Bible passage or the explanatory material you are studying. They work best when everyone has access to the same Bible translation. Enhance crossword puzzles by:

- Racing in teams of three to see who can finish first.
- Enlarging the puzzle so it covers the floor or table.
- Letting students give answers and tell why that fact matters.
- Guiding youth to create their own crossword puzzles and exchange with each other. Students will learn first by searching for questions and second by solving each other's crossword puzzles.

To create a crossword puzzle:

1. Circle key words in the passage (or commentary).
2. Write a brief definition for each word.
3. Arrange the words on graph paper so they cross. Start with the longest words. (If at first you don't succeed, keep rearranging.) Put one letter in each square.
4. Label the definitions in ACROSS and DOWN.
5. Recopy the crossword puzzle with no words filled in.

DECODE THE TRUTH

Junior highers are particularly fond of decoding and mystery solving. Watch for decoding ideas in newspapers, on cereal boxes, and in contests. Then write or draw Bible truths in those formulas. Even better, guide youth to create coded messages for each other. Possibilities include:

- **Maze:** Draw (or guide students to draw) a maze in which the right path passes through correct solutions and the wrong path presents worldly or wrong solutions.
- **A–Z:** Students write A to Z on one column and then Z to A in the other column. The matching letters give the code. Adapt for other formulas.
- **Circled letters** (called "Jumble" in some newspapers): Create four or five fill-in-the-blank questions. Circle letters in each answer to spell the key Bible truth. Challenge youth to fill in the blanks and unscramble the circled letters to discover the key Bible truth. HINT: This works best when all students have the same Bible translation.
- **Backward words:** Students must write words forward or hold them to a mirror to read them. Good choice for quick results.

● **Decoder wheel:** This sample gives a secret to success with parents. To discover the secret, youth write the letter under the arrow *(P)* and every second letter until they've gone around the circle twice.

DIARY ENTRIES

Youth put their most private thoughts into diaries or journals. Invite them to do the same during Bible study. Journaling encourages youth to put themselves into the Bible passage. Explain before youth write that they may choose not to share parts of their writing. Use assignments like those given under "Passing Notes." Also try:

● You are Mary and have just been told that you will bear God's child. You are 14. Write your thoughts and feelings in a diary entry. Include what you think your parents, friends, and boyfriend will say.

● Choose a character in the Parable of the Lost Son (Luke 15:11-32). Write a diary entry about your experiences and feelings.

VARIATION: Keep a journal for each session of a multi-session study.

FILL IN THE COMICS

Blank out the word bubbles from Sunday newspaper cartoons. Direct youth to apply the passage to present life by adding a new dialogue based on the Bible passage you're studying.

GUIDED PARAPHRASE

Paraphrase means "put into your own words." Rather than asking, "What does this passage mean to you?" ask it by guiding youth to paraphrase. It is usually best as an individual assignment, each student writing his or her own paraphrase and then reading all or part of it to the class. If you have limited time, assign a portion of the passage to each student and guide them to paraphase orally.

Paraphrase can be used several ways by giving different instructions.

● **Simple paraphrase:** Write Romans 5:1-5 in your own words. Use words that someone who had never been to church would understand.

● **Paraphrase by circumstances:** Write Matthew 6:19-23 as you would live it at the mall.

● **Personalized paraphrase:** Write about yourself fighting a series of temptations as Jesus did (Matthew 4:1-11).

VARIATION: Write several possible rewordings of the verse and instruct youth to choose the one they like best and tell why. You might find this done for you in your curriculum.

For example: Ephesians 5:21, "submit to one another out of reverence for Christ," could be paraphrased as these multiple choices.

a. _____ Putting others' needs first is a way to worship Christ.

b. _____ When it's hard to submit to someone I do it for Christ.

c. _____ Submitting becomes easier when we both do it.

d. _____ Jesus is my motivation for putting your needs first.

HANGMAN

Invite students to choose a phrase from the passage. Then guide them to write spaces for each letter of their phrase or word on the chalkboard. Challenge the others to guess it letter by letter. For each wrong guess, draw a part of the hanging man (usual order is head, neck, body, arm, arm, leg, leg). The initial goal is to guess the word or phrase before the man gets hanged. The ultimate goal is to enable youth to both teach and learn Bible concepts.

ADAPTATION: The show "Wheel of Fortune" is a version of hangman. Play it by awarding slips of paper worth 100 points for every guessed consonant. Sell vowels for 200 points.

HOUSE MAP

Guide youth to draw a map of their house or room and to label it in ways they can obey a Scriptural truth in those rooms. Examples include:

● Draw a floor plan and draw in five things in your house that matter to you. Read Matthew 6:33 and tell how putting Jesus first impacts these, changes their value, or guides their use.

● How does 1 Corinthians 13:4-7 impact how you act in each room of your house?

IDEA CHAINS

Challenge teams to make a chain of ideas longer than the other teams'. Give each team a stack of small paper, masking tape, and a marker. Direct them to write on each paper one idea that meets the assignment, then tape the papers end to end to make a chain. Youth love the competitive nature of this type of brainstorming. Sample assignments include:

● Name ways you can witness at school.
● Name specific ways to love your neighbor as yourself.
● Name temptations youth face.
● Name ways to resist temptation.
● Describe characteristics of a perfect date.

VARIATION: Each idea must begin with the last letter of the previous. Example: *W*itness with word*s*...*S*how faith with my actio*n*....

LETTERS

Pass out stationery and invite youth to write letters to apply the Bible passage. Possibilities include:

● **To Jesus:** Write a letter to Jesus talking with Him about how you will live a Bible command.

● **To a Bible character:** Write a letter to the writer of a Bible book asking for advice on a specific part of the passage. Example: "Paul—You say in 1 Corinthians 13:5 that love is not easily angered. I get furious with my boyfriend. Does this mean we aren't in love?" Exchange letters and answer as you think the writer of the Bible book would answer.

● **From a Bible character:** Write a letter home from one of the characters in the passage telling what happened, why you think it happened, and how your life is different because of it. Example: You are Leah and know your dad is planning to marry you off to someone who is in love with your sister (Genesis 29:16-30).

● **To a friend:** Write a letter to your friend about living a Bible command. Examples: Ask forgiveness; tell about Jesus.

● **Love letter:** Write a love letter to someone you like expressing the love qualities of 1 Corinthians 13:4-7 or another love passage. You will not have to mail the letter.

LISTENING SHEET

When you have a great amount of information that must be presented in a short time, give your students an incomplete outline and encourage them to fill in the blanks as you teach. Writing gets your students involved and increases their retention.

MAPS WITH MEANING

Maps can spell b-o-r-e-d-o-m. To cultivate youth's interest in maps:

• Use maps that have personal meaning, such as classroom, school, or home. Sample: Guide youth to draw every desk in one class, mark their own desk, and name ways they can minister to the people in the other desks.

• Get youth involved with Bible maps by writing on them, filling in details, illustrating events, tracing a journey.

• Cut the map into a puzzle, adding a piece each week.

• Miniaturize or enlarge the map to add to its appeal.

PASSING NOTES

Youth love to pass notes between classes and during church. Put this practice to great use by directing them to write notes as part of their Bible study. For example,

• If you were one of Daniel's friends in the fiery furnace, what note would you pass to your friend the next day? Find the details in Daniel 3:8-30. Be sure to include what got you into the furnace in the first place, the scary parts, and the happy ending.

• How would you have felt the next day after you and your brothers threw Joseph into the pit and then changed your mind and sold him? Write a note to a good friend telling what happened and how you feel about it. Find the details in Genesis 37:17-28.

POETRY FOR EVERYONE

Poetry can express Bible truth in a clear and easy-to-remember way. It can communicate feelings such as security, assurance, oneness with Christ, and other crucial faith foundations. Provide a form so youth who do not usually write poetry can succeed. Suggest that students feel free to use any other form they prefer. Samples:

• **Limerick:** A limerick has two long lines that rhyme, followed by two short lines that rhyme, followed by a fifth long line that rhymes with the first two. Limericks can express Bible themes or introduce youth to one another (or to you). To write a limerick, guide youth to write the characteristics of the Bible theme or person and then arrange them in limerick form. This example introduced a dear friend who raises roses and teaches a girls' Sunday School class:

There once was a woman named Josie.
Who said she would brag on her roses.
But they had black spot,
So she decided to not,
And instead teaches girls about Moses.

- **Describe the topic:**

_____

(Theme word such as "Resurrection")

_____   _____

(Two adjectives describing the theme word)

_____   _____   _____

(Three action words describing how to live the theme word)

_____   _____   _____   _____

(Four-word phrase describing the effect of the theme word)

_____

(One word that means the same as the theme)

Sample:

Resurrection
Amazing   Freeing
Obey   Smile   Triumph
Fear death no more
Life

- **Write a new verse:** Choose a familiar poem like "Roses are Red" and add a new verse on the truth of the Bible passage.

RECIPE/PRESCRIPTION

Distribute recipe cards (or a mock prescription pad) and invite youth to tell you the recipe (or prescription) for solving a certain problem or creating a certain good situation. Base your assignment on the passage. Examples:

- Write the recipe for acceptable speech (Ephesians 4:29).
- Write the recipe for joy (Philippians passages).
- Write a prescription for solving conflicts (Matthew 18:15-20).

ROAD SIGN

Provide colored markers and direct youth to tear or draw the shape of the road sign that tells how to live or how they have lived the

Bible principle you are studying. Road sign possibilities include: Stop, Crossing, Yield, Caution, Sharp Curve, Danger, Detour. Sample questions:

- How would you have responded to the serpent in the garden?
- What advice would you give someone about to enter high school?
- How have you responded to Jesus' call to follow Him in the past?
- What sign describes your spiritual status right now?
- How do you want to respond in the future?

VARIATION: Make a set of road signs for each youth. Read a passage such as the Ten Commandments, Colossians 3, or James 1. Invite students to hold up their signs during the reading to show their response.

SELF REPORT CARD

"Do you live the Christian life?" This question cannot be answered "yes" or "no." Report cards they complete themselves can help your students assess their own progress and discern areas for improvement. Topics that work well with report cards include spiritual gifts (Ephesians 4; Romans 12; 1 Corinthians 12), fruit of the Spirit (Galatians 5:22-23), the Ten Commandments (Exodus 20:1-17), new life vs. old life (Colossians 3), the Sermon on the Mount (Matthew 5–7).

VARIATION: Instruct youth to leave their cards in their chairs with their names at the top. Direct them to find and mark one quality on each classmate's card for which they could give an *A*. Repeat, instructing them to find and mark on each card a *B* quality (present but needs improving). The third time, instruct youth to find and mark a *C* (not present yet or needs much improvement). Note that one person may give one an *A* for for the same quality another gives a *C* or *B*. Encourage compassion rather than cutting. Ask, "How might you bring your *C* to an *A?*" "What makes you surprised about *A's?*"

VARIATION: Guide youth to grade themselves on undesirable qualities, like the acts of the sinful nature (Ephesians 5:19-21). In this case, *F's* are great!

VARIATION: Give grades to TV shows, movies, and magazines.

STICKERS

Invite youth to write their responses to a Bible truth on stickers. Create stickers with adhesive paper available in school supply cata-

logs or by cutting standard white name tags. Or let students create the stickers in the shape they feel communicates their assignment. Sample assignments:
- Create a symbol, sign, or face that communicates this passage.
- What color/shape/direction/mood does this passage suggest?
- Summarize this passage in one phrase on your sticker.

TEACHER REPORT CARD
Periodically (perhaps at report card time) let your students evaluate you. Give each a report card and invite them to give you letter grades with pluses and minuses just like at school. Encourage comments. Sample:

```
                    TEACHER REPORT CARD
_____ Makes the Bible clear
_____ Gives me a chance to discover answers for myself
_____ Shows how faith applies to everyday life
_____ Uses words I understand
_____ Helps me correct mistakes without making me feel dumb
_____ Gives good advice
_____ Keeps class interesting
_____ Shows Christlike actions and attitudes
_____ Demonstrates love for me and other youth

My favorite part about class is: _____
What I'd most like changed is: _____

Comments: _____
```

TELEPHONE NUMBERS
Help youth remember the location of a Bible passage or the truth of that passage by putting it in phone number form. Like regular phone numbers, words or letters can be used. Let your students' imaginations run wild. All they need are seven letters, numbers, or syllables. Samples:
- Reach God any time at Jeremiah 33:3 (Jer-e-mi-ah is the first four).
- Learn how to love by dialing 1-John4V728 (1 John 4:7-8).
- Real power available at PHI-L413 (Phil. 4:13).

● When you feel far from God, call unto Him: 2 Chron. 7:14-16.

THERMOMETER

To evaluate a single characteristic such as a forgiving attitude, willingness to obey God, or toleration of fellow believers, guide each student to draw a thermometer. Let them decide their own "degree marks." Perhaps they would divide the thermometer into fourths for "always, usually, seldom, never" or into tenths for percent.

T-SHIRT MOTTO

Distribute large paper cut in T-shirt shapes or use actual T-shirts and fabric markers. Direct youth to put in their own words one phrase from the passage you are studying. Good passages for this include John 14:1-21 and Matthew 5–7. Encourage youth to add a logo, design, or symbol that matches the saying. If you use cloth T-shirts, encourage youth to wear them. If you use paper, display them.

VARIATION: Create hats that communicate a role, a Bible character's personality, or a favorite Bible verse.

WANT AD

Guide students to define characteristics or qualities of Christianity with a want ad. Give each paper, sample want ads, and pencils. Possibilities include:

● Write an ad for a faithful believer based on Hebrews 11.

● Write an ad for a Christian who acts the same at school and church. Base it on James 1–2. Explain why hypocrisy won't work in this job.

● Write an ad for a prophet based on the Book of Amos (or whatever character you are studying).

WHY GOD SAYS SO

Direct one team of youth to list the reasons TO obey a biblical guideline and another team to list the reasons NOT TO obey the rule. Senior highers generated these lists:

Why should we wait until marriage to have sex?
1. God says so.
2. Can get sexually transmitted diseases.
3. Virginity is a great wedding present.
4. Makes marriage more special.
5. I'd be jealous if my spouse had already had sex.

6. Can die from AIDS.
7. I'd feel better about myself.
8. People respect you more, including the one you marry.
9. Virginity is something to be proud of.
10. Marriage is a great place to learn how to have sex.
11. Kids cost money and I don't have much.
12. When I talk to people who aren't virgins I say, "Any day I could become like you, but you can never become like me."

Why should I have sex before marriage?
1. It feels good.
2. I have trouble waiting.
3. I can't get a date any other way.
4. I don't want to be called frigid.

If the "disobedient" team wins, point out the weakness of human reasoning. Or highlight the power of one reason over another.

WORD BUBBLES
Rather than giving students paper with a question at the top, enclose the question in a word bubble and leave a blank word bubble for the answer. This simple variation encourages less stained-glass language and more real-life talk.

ADAPTATION: Using other interesting writing spaces, like the "glass" of a magnifying glass or the brain of a thinking Christian.

PLUS...
Consider offering these other options to your students:
- Make a greeting card for a Bible character in crisis or joy.
- Create a logo that communicates the Bible passage.
- Write a monologue, dialogue, or play.
- Create a tombstone for Eve, Moses, Jezebel, John, yourself, etc.
- Choose from many words the one that best expresses truth.
- Make a time line or illustrate an existing one.
- Make a mobile with symbols and illustrations from the passage.
- Test yourself before and after the study.
- Respond anonymously to a lesson (privacy encourages honesty).
- Make transparencies for the overhead projector.
- Make bookmarks with Bible verses or paraphrases.
- Write a litany or responsive prayer.
- Outline the Bible passage or Bible book.
- Write a biography of a Bible character.

8
Talk Starters

The One Who Talks Is the One Who Learns

Rationale: Teenagers love to talk. Even shy kids will talk when they feel safe and listened to. As your students talk, they solidify their beliefs and understand their faith. As they voice ideas, they have opportunity to evaluate those ideas. As youth share their personal experiences with friends, problems, and activities, they discover that the Bible is the source of better friendships, solved problems, and fun activities. As youth talk about the Bible, the Bible becomes a comfortable friend and a way to listen to God. The ideas in this chapter help your students make these exciting discoveries.

Teaching Tip: Encourage youth to talk by finding something in every response that you agree with. Even totally wrong answers can be affirmed with, "I see how you drew your conclusions." When students' answers and experiences are accepted, they feel accepted and venture talking again. When you care about youth, they feel God must care.

Teaching Tip: Probably the single most effective talking tool is a prop. Its value for increasing the success of discussions cannot be overestimated. A prop is something students hold, make, or do during the discussion. Props make it easier for youth to focus on the discussion, motivate them to listen to each other, and invite participation. Props become more effective as they become more novel. Novel doesn't have to mean complicated: write on a paper plate rather than a piece of paper. For suggestions of props and how to use them, see "Life Deck," "Paper Plate Feelings," "Picture Response," "Predicament Cubes," "Prop Ideas," and "Toss the Yarn" in this chapter.

Teaching Tip: What youth talk about is not always what they believe. As you lead discussions, realize that talking is a way to try on ideas and to discover whether the ideas are true. Rather than acting shocked, guide youth to think through their ideas with Bible facts and supportive information. As youth do their own talking, they discover that God's ways really do work. Let youth do more talking than you do so they can develop a strong faith based on firm study of the Bible.

Bonus Section: Rules for Effective Talking Teenagers will talk when they feel safe and smart. Enhance this by introducing these rules in your group, emphasizing the reason for each:

1. When someone talks, listen and understand.
2. No laughing at or ridiculing what anyone says or feels.
3. When you disagree, do so agreeably.
4. When someone makes a mistake, affirm your love.
5. On "everybody participates" questions, each person gives an answer.

ADVANTAGE/DISADVANTAGE

While discussing what to do about a dilemma, guide youth to list possible solutions and then take turns telling an advantage and a disadvantage of each solution. This helps youth look at decisions from more than one side, as well as to see that all decisions cost, whether for the world or for God. The ultimate goal is that youth notice that God's advantages are worth the cost. For example: *"Should I have sex before marriage?"*

- Yes, because most other people do.
  Advantage: Get lots of dates.
  Disadvantage: Have to worry about AIDS or getting pregnant.
- Yes, because I am in love.
  Advantage: I can express my love physically; feels good.
  Disadvantage: Tends to destroy a relationship.
- No, because God said so.
  Advantage: Feel good about decision and relationship with God.
  Disadvantage: Get labeled a prude or a cold fish.
- No, for the sake of my happiness in marriage.
  Advantage: I'll know my spouse and I share something I never shared with anyone else.
  Disadvantage: Hard to wait until marriage to express sex.

VARIATION: Use this with television shows. Rather than asking,

"Is this a good show?" invite youth to name three positives and three negatives.

AGREE/DISAGREE

Many Bible truths are like diamonds: they have many facets of truth. To bring out these facets, guide your students to talk with one another in a session of Agree/Disagree. Post four signs: AGREE, DISAGREE, STRONGLY AGREE, STRONGLY DISAGREE.

Direct youth to stand in the middle of the room. Read a statement about the Bible passage. Point out the signs and instruct youth to move to the sign that tells how they feel about the statement.

Ask members of each group to explain their choices, beginning with the smallest group. After talking with all four groups, show how each comment brings out some aspect of truth.

Bring youth back to the center and repeat with the next statement.

This method is basically a walking discussion. The movement invites participation in talking. Calling on someone different each time gives everyone opportunity to express an insight.

These examples aid the discussion of Matthew 6:5-8:

- Praying in public is mostly for show (vv. 5-6).
- Private prayer is the best way to talk to God (v. 6).
- Short prayers are better than long ones (v. 7).
- Because God knows what we need, we don't need to pray (v. 8).

COMPARE

Comparison helps youth notice how and why Bible truth works. Guide youth to compare the Bible passage to something that happens today— "If Jesus gave a Sermon on the Mount at your school today, what would He emphasize?" Guide youth to compare a Bible character to themselves or someone else, or to compare one Bible truth to a seeming opposite one to discover how they harmonize— "Why does James say 'Faith without works is dead' (2:26) and Paul emphasize that 'Righteousness that comes by faith' (Romans 4:13)?"

COMPETITION

Youth will do almost anything with more vigor if they are competing against another team. Let your teams be no larger than four to ensure everyone's participation. Samples include:

- Name more reasons to obey God than any other team.
- Name more things to praise God for than the other team.

- List more ways to love a friend than any other team.
- Name more things you like about the other team.

FIND THE OPPOSITE

To guide youth to discover how to obey God and why disobeying God is painful, direct them to find the opposite. For "thou shalt nots" guide youth to list how to obey God. These are from Colossians 3:5:

The opposite of . . .	*is . . .*
sexual immorality	being loyal to my marriage even before I'm married
impurity	being real myself and demanding it of others
lust	seeing people as people, not objects
evil desires	wanting the best for people
greed	generosity
idolatry	keeping God in first place and in command

For do's, list the consequences of not obeying God. These are from Colossians 3:12:

The opposite of . . .	*is . . .*
compassion	using people
kindness	hurting feelings
humility	know-it-all-ness
gentleness	brutality
patience	anxiety, worry

This process helps youth to see the reason for God's prohibitions and the "yes" behind God's every "no."

VARIATION: Direct youth to rewrite the Ten Commandments without "no" or "not." One of my favorites, written by a high school junior for "Thou shalt not commit adultery," was "Do it with your spouse and keep it in your house."

FINISH THE SENTENCE

Guide your students to express how the Bible passage applies to their lives by completing sentence fragments you provide. Samples:

- This passage makes me want to . . .
- I think it would be hard to obey this passage because . . .
- I think God wants me to change . . .
- I think God is proud that I . . .
- I most admire _____ in this passage because . . .
- I am like the person in this passage because . . . but different because . . .

FOUR WORDS, TWO WORDS, ONE WORD

Invite your students to summarize the truth of the passage or verse in four words. Then guide them to summarize it in two. Finally invite them to choose the one key word (or substitute a word that means the same).

VARIATION: Ask the first few youth to use four words, the next few two words, and the last few one word.

VARIATION: Assign a word in the passage to each youth, then challenge them to find it and tell why it is important to the passage.

I WISH

"I Wish" is a form of sentence completion that encourages youth to pinpoint areas they want to change. The Scripture itself becomes the source of answers, methods, and plans for change. Use "I Wish" to begin a discussion on how to apply the Bible passage.

Begin with a fill-in-the-blank sentence. Write the sentence on paper or the chalkboard to help youth focus on their answers rather than on remembering the sentence. Choose one of the following samples and then challenge students to find verses in your passage to help them fulfill their wishes.

- I wish I could stop before I give in to temptation of _____ .
- I wish I could recognize the destructiveness of words like _____ before I say them.
- I wish I could overcome my worry about _____ .
- I wish my home were more _____ .
- I wish I were more _____ .

INTENTIONS

As you encounter Bible characters in your study, encourage youth to identify characters' questions and actions and what they think the characters' intentions were. This process guides youth to see the consequences of decisions by talking about other people's decisions and motivations. Point out that they can avoid the Bible characters' mistakes and imitate their successes.

LIFE DECK

Prepare a deck of cards, writing one life area to a card: SCHOOL, FAMILY, CHURCH, FRIENDSHIP, DATING, HOME, PLAYING SPORTS, WATCHING SPORTS, FREE TIME, CLOTHES, MONEY, TELEVISION. To use them:

• **Option #1:** Display the cards upside down and direct each student to choose one. Invite them to apply the Bible principle you are studying with an explanation or a 30-second speech.

• **Option #2:** Challenge youth to arrange the cards in the order of importance or ease of action. Examples: Where is it easier to forgive? At school or home? In what area does Jesus want you to focus your talking time? Your praying time? Your understanding time?

• **Option #3:** Guide youth to give themselves a grade on how well they live for God in each life area, specifically as relates to the Bible theme.

VARIATION: Make a deck of cards specifically related to your theme. For example, if you are studying how Jesus responded to suffering, make a deck listing social, emotional, and physical ills.

LIFE LETTER

As each student enters, give him or her an official-looking letter on church stationery. Watch for reactions and discreetly jot down comments to share later. Call for discussion prompted by the letter. Sample:

Dear Church Member:

Your share of the expenses of the ministry and upkeep of_____ Church is $380.64 per year. This may be paid in one lump sum or be divided into fifty-two (52) equal payments of $7.32. These payments are due beginning January 1, 1992.

If the first month's payments are not received by February 1, you will be summoned to appear before the Stewardship Committee to explain your willful neglect of your God-given obligation. See 2 Corinthians 8:1-12.

Questions that could be used include: What is your first reaction to this letter? What is a better way to motivate giving? Why should we give to the church? What should we do when people refuse to give anything to the church or when they take more than they give?

LIKE/UNLIKE

Guide youth to understand Bible concepts by telling what they are like and not like. Post these sentence fragments and guide youth to fill them in:

• God (or heaven, or whatever your theme) is like _____ because . . .

● God (or heaven, or whatever your theme) is not like _____ because . . .

Samples:

● God is like a blanket because He makes me feel cozy, but He is not like a blanket because He really can keep the bad guys away at night.

● Heaven is like home because I will feel happy there, but it is not like home because no fire or robber can hurt it.

● Forgiveness is like freedom because it brings back a relationship, but it is not like freedom because not everybody wants it.

VARIATION: Guide youth to tell how they are like or not like a Bible character, or how they live or don't live according to the lesson's theme.

MY FAVORITE WORD

Provide several words or phrases that describe or summarize the passage. Invite youth to choose their favorite and tell why. Their talking frequently brings out insights never before noticed.

MY OWN PARABLE

Jesus used everyday objects and experiences to explain spiritual truths—we call them parables. After studying one of Jesus' parables, invite youth to use an everyday object to tell their own parable about the theme.

These examples were generated by a group of tenth-grade boys studying Matthew 13:18-52 and Mark 4:1-34:

● Sin is like pizza. It tastes great at first, then it's bad (indigestion).

● Sin is like an ink pen—it works at first but when it's empty you have nothing.

● The kingdom of heaven is like an apple orchard—there are bad apples among the good for a while.

● Sin is like a spider web—you're attracted to its sparkle but get all trapped in it, and the sticky feeling stays a long time.

OBJECT TALK

Object lessons can make the truth clear and memorable. Guide youth to do their own object lessons by placing in the center of the table several objects or pictures that relate to the passage or theme you are studying. Invite youth to choose one and tell how it explains the passage or relates to the story. For Luke 15 you might present a tax document; a coin; a toy calf; a toy pig; and pictures of a boy, a dad, and a big brother.

VARIATION: Let students create their own object lessons from clothes they are wearing or something they brought with them in a billfold or purse.

PANEL DISCUSSION

Enlist two to four members of your group, or people they respect, to serve on a panel. Good panel discussions are short, involve the audience heavily, and use people who are more interested in answering questions than making speeches. To increase the success:

● Use topics already interesting to youth: a panel of guys and girls to talk about what guys like in girls and vice versa; a panel of teachers to suggest how to please a teacher; a panel of kids and parents who get along to explain how to make a happy home.

● Plant a few audience participation questions to get discussion rolling.

● Use the panel early in your session so you can let it go on if interest is high or move on to other things when interest wanes.

PAPER PLATE FEELINGS

Instead of just asking, "How do you feel when you are lonely?" give students paper plates and pencils. Direct them to write on the outside how they look to other people when they are lonely and to write on the inside how they look to themselves. As youth show and talk about the plates, they answer the question. It takes a little longer than asking the question, but the quality of response is better and more honest.

Use this technique with any feeling—fear, excitement, worry, anger, infatuation, love, forgiveness, grief, repentance, and more.

PICTURE RESPONSE

Gather photographs, illustrations, or cartoons that relate to your theme. Display them and invite students to react to them;

● How do you think this person would react to today's passage?

● What does this person need from Jesus? From you?

● What advice would you give this person based on our passage?

Notice that when youth talk about pictures, they often talk about themselves. The more specific the solutions for the "picture person," the better your students are helped.

ADAPTATION: Let students draw the pictures or take photographs.

PREDICAMENT CUBES

When your curriculum includes case studies or you want to talk about how to apply a principle to real life, create predicament cubes. Use any square box—photo cubes are ideal—or make your own like the following sample. Tape one predicament or case study to each side and invite students to roll the cube. The roller reads the predicament on top and suggests ways to apply the Bible verses to it.

VARIATION: Create a second cube with principles from the passage you are studying. Roll the cubes together and ask how the Bible principle addresses the predicament. Make sure each principle applies to each predicament so that solutions are all appropriate.

VARIATION: Leave one side blank and invite players to suggest a predicament or solution from their own lives. Give the option to roll again if they would rather not share a personal situation.

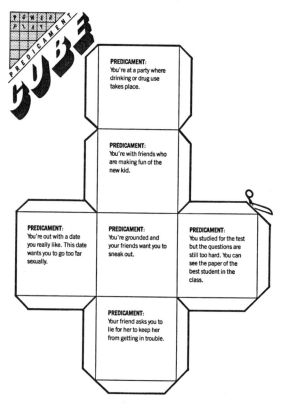

PROP IDEAS
Use a telephone for talking to God or for giving advice to a friend. Use square of toilet paper for naming ways to clean up the messes in our lives. How might you use these props to make your Bible lesson clearer?

- facial tissues
- clock
- money
- paper cups
- clay
- light bulb
- timer
- set of keys
- plant

PROVE ME WRONG
Play "devil's advocate" and challenge youth to prove you wrong with truths from the Bible or their experience. This is particularly effective on truths youth resist. When they have to do the convincing rather than the rebelling, they tend to convince themselves. Possibilities include:

- Prove the value of abstinence with, "It's OK to take a drink or two at a party as long as I don't get drunk."
- Prove the value of obeying God with, "God won't mind if I sin once in a while."
- Prove the fact of the Resurrection with, "Jesus didn't really rise from the dead—that's just what our Sunday School teachers have taught us all our lives."

Devil's advocate also works well on wrong statements like:

- Obeying Christ takes away all your fun.
- Becoming a Christian means I have to give up too much.
- Jesus doesn't know what life is like today.
- God's will and my hopes, dreams, and plans are always opposite.

SOMETHING I LIKE/SOMETHING I DON'T LIKE
To enhance youth's evaluative skills and help them take steps toward solidifying their beliefs, guide them to share something they like and don't like about a viewpoint or statement. This has three values:

1. Youth can answer this question. It starts them talking.
2. Personal impressions can be hints of truth or falsehood.
3. Youth gripe less when they look for a good with every bad.

Use this for evaluating statements about Scripture. Possibilities:

- If you're a Christian, God will bless you with money and health.
- Suffering is part of the Christian life.
- Praising God makes everything better.

ADAPTATION: When evaluating Scripture itself, change the assignment to "Something I find easy to obey/Something I resist obeying."

SOMETHING RIGHT/SOMETHING WRONG

When studying temptation, cults, spiritual deception, or other themes with half truths, invite students to spot something right and something wrong with certain statements or actions. This heightens youth's discernment of falsehood while acknowledging the appeal of many half truths.

VARIATION: Challenge youth to evaluate their magazines, TV shows, or music with this method.

TALK TO GOD

Many teenagers feel uncomfortable praying aloud. Give your students prayer practice by praying during class. Rather than limiting prayer to the end or beginning, pray at different times each week. Cultivate the habit of pausing to pray whenever a need or joy arises. Explain that prayer is communicating with God and involves both talking and listening. Prayer formats include:

• **Popcorn prayer:** Youth pop in a sentence whenever it comes to them.

• **Prayer lists:** List requests and praises on paper or orally. Then pray about them. Explain that simply talking about these can be prayer.

• **Celebration:** Share good things as praise to God.

• **Partners:** Pray in partners, sharing concerns and then praying for each other's concerns. This allows more detailed sharing.

• **Prayer in the hat:** Write prayer requests on papers and place them in a hat or box. Take turns drawing from the hat and praying for that need. This allows the anonymity that encourages honesty.

• **Prayer chain:** When needs arise during the week, each student calls another until all are praying.

• **Notes to God:** Because many youth find it easier to write notes than talk, guide them to write a note to God.

• **Dialogue:** Guide students to write a prayer dialogue beginning with their words and writing what they think God says back or write a dialogue between God and a Bible character.

• **Listening:** Because prayer includes listening, guide youth to write one prayer entirely from God to them. Enforce silence for this.

VARIATIONS: See "Manual for Christian Living" (chapter 11).

TEENAGERS SAY...

Help your students feel freer to answer by using the technique Jesus used in Matthew 16:13: He began by asking what other people said about Him and then asked their own viewpoint. Youth feel safer answering generally: "Teenagers think that..." rather than "I think...." Amazingly, when you ask, "What do teenagers say/think/feel about...," students give their own opinions.

10-SECOND TESTIMONIES

Invite youth to talk for 10 to 30 seconds about how a specific principle has influenced their lives. Ten seconds is long enough to say something significant but short enough not to intimidate. Interrupt at the 10-second point (fudge a little if a shy speaker has just gotten going).

ADAPTATION: Some students may have more to say after the first round. Allow another 10 seconds until everyone who wants a second turn has one. Then allow more turns until all have said as much as they want.

Topics for which 10-second testimonies work well include:

- How is your life different since you became a Christian?
- What difference does your faith make at school?
- How does Jesus make a difference in how you solve problems?
- How did the retreat change your life?
- How has forgiveness brought closeness with someone?
- Tell about something neat you've learned recently during a sermon.

30-SECOND SPEECHES

Explain that everyone will talk for 30 seconds on a topic that relates to the day's Bible study. (For instance, how to live out one of the Beatitudes.) Write the topics on cards and let students draw a speech topic without looking, or let them choose their favorite. Point out sources of ideas such as the Bible passage, personal experience, or the student book. Call on volunteers until all speak. Downplay the "impromptu speech" aspect and build up "talking"; talking is more comfortable than "making a speech."

ADAPTATION: Use speeches for openings when you want kids to focus on a need or question the Bible passage can meet. Use them for closing when you want kids to think about applying the Bible passage.

TOSS THE YARN

This familiar technique is new to many of today's youth. Those who are familiar with it still find it appealing: they know it means honest discussion on a topic important to them. Seat the group in one large circle. Hold a ball of yarn. Explain that only the person holding the yarn can speak. Introduce the topic and give your comment briefly. Hold one end and toss it to someone across the circle. That person now speaks on the topic, holds a corner of yarn, and tosses the ball to another person. Continue until everyone has spoken. Then invite any who have something else to say to raise their hand. Toss to them.

Themes that work well with yarn sharing:
- How I have grown in Christ as a result of this Bible study.
- What makes me depressed and what do I do about it.
- What I like about our group.
- One thing I could do to make our group more Christlike.
- How the Ten Commandments impact my life.

Use the ball also for compliments and affirmation:
- Toss the ball to someone who has helped you grow in Christ and tell how. (Be certain *everyone* gets the ball at least once.)
- Give compliments to the one holding the ball. (The one with the ball stays silent and all others talk.)

Use the web that forms in the circle for questions like:
- What does the yarn in the middle teach us about our topic?
- How is our group like what we see in the middle of the circle?
- How do our daily lives show this kind of connectedness to people?

WHAT IF?

Guide youth to think through dilemmas they face with these steps:

1. List all the worries the group has by calling them out spontaneously. Call these "what if's." (What if my mom dies? What if I fail geometry?)

2. Divide the "what if's" among the group. Next to each, write what you could do about it, especially as guided by the passage(s) you're studying.

3. Discuss the solutions and suggest ways you might prevent some of the problems and how to cope with the ones you can't prevent. Point out that just knowing what we'd do can give some relief from worry. Emphasize that God will get us through every "what if."

WORD ASSOCIATION

Challenge youth to write the first word that comes to their mind when they hear a theme word. Get the association process rolling with neutral words like hot (cold) and young (old). Invite youth to share what they wrote and why. Affirm a wide variety of responses, pointing out how each comment helps us understand the topic. Then open to the Bible passage to discover even more.

Good themes for word association include mercy, forgiveness, crucifixion, obedience, cross, Satan, temptation.

PLUS ...

Consider these other options for teaching your Bible passage:

- Retelling (similar to paraphrase or memorizing);
- Book or article report;
- Group lecture (youth combine and present their knowledge);
- Problem solving (list options, evaluate, choose the best);
- Guest speakers (ones who communicate and relate well to youth);
- Commercials (even better when youth create props; see chapter 10);
- Compliment bombardment (group compliments each member);
- Media evaluation (see chapter 10 for sample questions);
- Say what you want your obituary to read and how to make it so;
- 90-second lecture (limit your lectures, let youth time you);
- Youth give each other pep talks (Hebrews 10:24-25 in action);
- Listening teams (as you lecture, each listens for something specific).

9
Art and Drama

Art Encourages the Involvement That Produces Learning

Rationale: Art demands involvement. When fingers move to dramatize, draw, doodle, or dabble, minds concentrate. When Bible truth is communicated through art, learning occurs in these ways:
- The artist remembers what he or she created;
- The observer remembers the art presented because sight, sound, and movement are involved.

You may be a teacher who (like me) shies away from art. Overcome your hesitation for the sake of your students. Each time you venture teaching the Bible with art, notice the insight your students present. To introduce a study on Jesus' view of divorce, I gave my senior highers a lump of clay and instructed them to shape it like someone feels when divorce occurs. Rand, usually very well behaved, threw his against the wall. Very upset, I said, "What are you doing?" Evenly, he replied, "You feel smashed against the wall when your parents announce their divorce." He was right. And I've never forgotten that truth.

Teaching Tip: When giving an art assignment, explain that the meaning of the art is much more important than the finished product. Don't say the art doesn't matter or you risk stifling the creativity of your artistic students. But don't let pressure to produce a polished work inhibit less artistic students from expressing their ideas.

ACT WITH SUNGLASSES
Keep pairs of plastic or paper sunglasses in your teaching materials. Youth tend to feel safer behind a pair of fake glasses and will say or dramatize things they might never do without them. Consider the

many things you can do with sunglasses:

• Give plain paper glasses and invite students to decorate them to communicate the theme of the day: seeing the good in people; seeing people as Jesus does; looking for opportunities to demonstrate faith; seeing chances to witness.

• Direct all to wear their glasses and tell how they "see the need for forgiveness," or "look beneath the surface for real needs."

• Distribute dark glasses and ask such questions as: What are we blind to? What do we hide behind? When do we walk in darkness rather than light? How does Jesus change the way we see the world?

ADD A FACE

Invite an artistic youth to draw the characters of the story for you ahead of class. Duplicate the drawing and instruct students to draw the facial expressions at each stage of the story.

ADAPTATION: Do the same thing with simple ovals. Some youth will add simple faces; others will embellish theirs with hair, bodies, and clothes.

CARTOON CREATING

Challenge students to draw a cartoon illustrating the truths discovered in the Bible passage. Cartoons will range from simple to complex in the same class. Each is equally valuable because the ideas are what count. Do praise those with detailed drawings just as you would a youth who expresses himself or herself well with words. Possibilities include:

• Illustrate how to do one of Jesus' Sermon on the Mount commands (Matthew 5–7). Use two or more frames.

• Draw how you look when you get angry in the first frame. Draw what Ephesians 4:26-27, 29-32 says to do about it in subsequent frames.

• Read a case study and draw how you think God would advise you to solve it based on the passages for the day.

CLAY SHAPING

Give each youth a lump of clay to shape the theme of your Bible passage. Sample themes which have worked well include temptation, sanctification, letting anger lead to sin, forgiveness, friendship, repentance, hope, fellowship.

More specific instructions might include:

- Shape what you think you'll see or feel when Jesus comes back.
- Mold what you do when a friend hurts you.
- Form how Adam and Eve felt after eating the forbidden fruit.

This method takes repeated encouragement but is well worth it. Try words like, "What do you think about when I mention forgiveness?" "How might you shape the feelings it brings?" "Keep squishing the clay, an idea will come." Explain, "Your shape can be literal or symbolic—for friendship you might shape two people talking or you might shape two rings that link."

When youth have all shaped their clay, invite each to share, beginning with volunteers. Point out spiritual insight in each.

HINT: Use play clay that doesn't rub off on hands, clothes, or the church. The wilder the colors, the better youth tend to like it.

ADAPTATION: Let youth keep their clay throughout the session to squish and mold. This absorbs energy and helps students focus on the discussion. The condition for keeping the clay is that youth not throw or pass the clay and the clay must stay in one piece.

DOODLE SHEET

Especially if your students doodle all over everything you give, provide jot sheets. Challenge youth to doodle on this sheet every truth or insight they hear. Award a group hug to the one who finds the most or produces the most insightful doodles during the session. Use creative borders or idea-starters around the jot sheets. Enlist your doodlers to create these.

DRAW ANYTIME

Whenever you assign a written response, offer the option to draw the response. Many youth pack more in a picture than words can say.

DRAW THE PASSAGE

Assign each youth one or more verses to illustrate. Because visual images can be easier to remember than words, students will remember the passage.

Students might illustrate in rebus form in which every word or phrase is represented by an image (see "Rebus" in chapter 12). Or youth might use a single image that summarizes the whole verse, as in political cartoons or simple illustrations.

ADAPTATION: Guide youth to draw an image or illustration of how they would live the passage in their own lives.

FINISH THE DOODLE
Provide youth with a beginning doodle, perhaps a shape or squiggle. Challenge them to complete it so it shows the truth of the passage.

MASKS
Guide youth to combine dabbling, drawing, and doodling with acting by creating masks, which can be as simple as paper and marker or as complex as a 3-D sculpture of papers, objects, and paints. The sense of anonymity a mask provides can free your students from inhibitions as they act.

MURAL/FRIEZE/GRAFFITI
Place a large sheet of paper on the wall, floor, or table and invite your group to respond to your lesson theme using words, symbols, and illustrations. For long dramatic passages like those in the Old Testament, assign a portion to each pair of youth and direct them to illustrate it. Assemble in the correct order in a frieze or mural. Encourage cartooning.

HINT: Youth like these best when everyone works at once rather than one writing while the others watch.

NAME TAGS
Let your name tags be part of the teaching process. Try these instructions:

● Make a name tag that shows a characteristic you think Jesus wants you to express.

● Tear your name tag into a symbol of this passage. For example, a house could remind you to invite people home to study the Bible like Priscilla and Aquila.

● Tear your name tag to show how you are like the Bible character in our study.

● Choose a phrase from this passage and tear your name tag to show how you will live it.

PAPER CUP, FOIL, PIPE CLEANER, OR PAPER CLIP SHAPING
Use anything moldable or tearable for meaningful dabbling. Where possible let the material match your theme. Tear paper cups into the shape of the theme of the passage. Mold foil into a way to reflect Jesus. Bend paper clips into a way you think Jesus wants to shape you.

Assignments that work well with **cups** include:

● Shape how you felt the last time someone was sarcastic with you or criticized you. After all have shared, instruct youth to pretend the person has apologized. Direct them to return their cups to original form. Obviously the cups will still have wrinkles or tears. Use this to point out the importance of using words positively in the first place—some damage cannot be repaired (Ephesians 4:29).

● Invite youth to list several sins. Direct them to choose one and shape the effect it has on the sinner or the one sinned against. After all have shared, explain that all these sinners have sought and received forgiveness from God. Direct youth to return the cups to their original shape. Tears and wrinkles will remain. Ask: Is it OK to sin since we can get forgiveness? Why is it better not to sin in the first place? Supplement by explaining that the effects of sin remain and that God's laws are meant to prevent trouble, not take away fun (Romans 6:1; Romans 1:20-32; John 10:10).

For **foil** try:

● While studying Gospel passages, give students foil and pens. Direct them to draw on or shape the foil to reflect a Christian attitude.

For **pipe cleaners** or **paper clips** try:

● Shape how people know you are a Christian. Insightful examples: Leave pipe cleaner straight to stay on the straight and narrow. Make paper clip round to show the unity of the group. Bend pipe cleaner up and down several times to show focusing on the up times rather than the down.

PAPER SHAPING

Provide markers and various colors, shapes, and textures of paper. Invite youth to express Bible truth in ways like these:

● Draw the colors of spirituality (or whatever your theme).
● Shape spirituality.
● Demonstrate the texture of spirituality.
● Make a hat that demonstrates spirituality.

PICTURE POEMS

Invite youth to draw the shape of the truth you're studying and then to write around that shape a description of or poem about that truth. For the Crucifixion, youth might draw a picture poem like the following.

```
            t
            o

            H
   My   sins   led
            s

            d
            e
            a
            t
            h
```

POSTER CREATION

Any time you add a visual, you enhance learning. Refuse to limit your posters to rectangles on the wall. Use various shapes and sizes and display them on the ceiling, on the floor, in the doorway, even on the backs of students. Posters are enhanced when students create them or write on the ones you created. Encourage cartoons, stick figures, and words and point youth to specific passages for support. Poster possibilities:

● Create a set of footprint posters telling the steps to becoming a Christian.

● Create a series of posters on how *not* to witness.

● Write questions inside flip posters that you must open to read.

● Cover your poster until time to use it to stimulate curiosity.

● Create a poster of a totally contemptible person. Then name ways to love this person.

● Use huge letter posters to spell out the theme of your study.

ROLE PLAY

A role play is a spontaneous drama during which at least one youth plays a role he does not usually assume. Popular possibilities are a parent, an enemy, someone with whom they conflict, a teacher, or even Jesus. Make role plays more interesting by putting them in a format different from "read off the paper." Possibilities include:

● **Spin a role play:** Draw a large circle on paper, divide it into pie shapes, and write a situation in each of the pie shapes. Attach a spinner with a small nail or thumb tack. Direct youth to spin and solve the case study the arrow lands on.

● **Twice:** Guide youth to role play twice: once in a way that's easy but causes more trouble; once in a way that really solves the problem.

• **Roll a box:** Tape a situation on each side of photo cube or square box and roll it. Act out the situation that comes to the top. See "Predicament Cubes" in chapter 8 for details.

• **Double role:** Roll two cubes, one with case studies, another with six attitudes or six family members. Direct youth to respond to the case study with that attitude or from the perspective of that family member.

Attitudes could include, cooperative, defensive, angry, curious, accusatory, open. Family members could be teenager, older sibling of teenager, father, mother, grandparent or other relative, younger sibling of teenager.

• **Two parts:** Give two separate youth their roles and bring them together with no former conversation.

Example:

Role 1: You borrowed your sister's favorite sweater without asking and spilled chocolate ice cream on it. The stain won't come out.

Role 2: You look in your drawer for your favorite sweater and discover it missing. When you go looking for it, you discover your sister has borrowed and stained it.

• **World problems:** Let the youth play leaders who have power to change world problems. Encourage one to act like an actual leader and the other to respond as they think God wants them to act, based on the passage.

• **Game board:** Write the situations on cards, stack them, and use them along with a board game to add interest.

SYMBOLS

Challenge youth to translate a Bible truth into symbols that will help them memorize it. If you're studying the healing at the pool of Bethesda, someone might draw a stick figure lying down and looking sad-faced. Then Jesus walks up. Then the man is standing and smiling. The truth drawn is, "In Jesus' power I can stand even with the most debilitating problem or illness." Another student might bring a "weeble" (the toy person that always rights itself) to show the same truth.

TANGRAM

A tangram is a square cut into seven shapes. The original tangram has two large triangles, three small triangles, a small square, and a trapezoid. Cut the square into these seven shapes or give students the freedom to cut their squares into any seven shapes. Then instruct students to arrange those shapes in a way that demonstrates the truth of that session. Their arrangements might show a symbol of the truth, a person in a certain position, a part of the body that can express that truth.

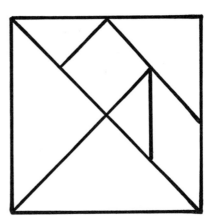

Though this may sound like playing, it forces students to think through the truth and express it in a concrete form.

USE THE PASSAGE AS YOUR SCRIPT

A wonderful way to get youth immediately involved with a passage is to act it out. Let youth use their Bibles as their scripts and you direct the action step-by-step. See samples under "Bible As Script" (chapter 4).

ADAPTATION: After acting out the passage from Scripture, invite youth to act it as it might occur today.

ADAPTATION: Divide the passage into scenes and guide youth to pose in tableau. The others name the verses they are posing.

WHAT IF I DO/WHAT IF I DON'T

Guide youth to act out two situations: first what would happen if they disobey the biblical principle you are studying, then what will happen if they obey the principle. Discuss with:

- Why does this principle work?
- What problems do we create by ignoring God?
- How are God's commands pointers toward happiness rather than prohibitors of fun?

PLUS . . .

Consider these other options for using art in your teaching:

- Photography;
- Collage;
- Montage (collection of pictures and words that relate to a theme);

- Interview someone who pretends to be a Bible character;
- Puppets;
- Tableau (still poses like nativity scenes);
- Film, video, or filmstrip evaluation (see evaluation questions under "Music Bible Study" in chapter 10);
    - Quality film or video that communicates the Bible truth;
    - Charades (of Bible actions, of attitudes, of Christlike love);
    - Pantomime (drama without words, sometimes narrated);
    - Monologue (drama with one person);
    - Dialogue between you and God; between a Bible person and God;
    - Write and perform plays, interpretations, and more;
    - Design a book cover for a book of the Bible or a biography of a Bible character;
    - Choral reading (also called reader's theater);
    - Comedy routine that communicates the theme of the passage;
    - Before and after cartoons on the difference Jesus, sanctification, or some other spiritual development makes.

10
Music

Music Enhances Bible Memory
and Expresses Bible Application

Rationale: The Bible says "make a joyful noise," not "create perfect music." Joy, not musical talent, is what counts when teaching with music. Let youth's natural love for music motivate them to study the Bible with it. Music can enhance Bible memory, convey Bible moods, and make Bible application relevant. As youth sing, write, and evaluate they remember, understand, and often experience Bible truth. Music also provides opportunity for musically talented youth to express Bible understanding in a way comfortable to them.

Teaching Tip: Emphasize a specific Bible passage with each music assignment. The goal of most music learning is to put Scripture phrases or paraphrases to music. When we don't focus on a specific passage, we force youth to draw on past knowledge and learn nothing new.

BRING A SONG
Hold a Bible study in which all you do is play, sing, and talk about your students' favorite Christian songs. This has these benefits:

- Songs are a comfortable way for teenagers to talk about God.
- Students encourage each other by sharing how the songs help them live their faith. They become the teachers.
- Youth learn that Christian music really can apply to everyday worries, can be of quality, and can be enjoyable.
- They discover ways music can express their beliefs.

Invite all your students to bring their favorite Christian song with the words written on large paper. The song can be a hymn, a contemporary Christian song, or something they composed. (Be sure to arrange for a way to play the music.) Encourage those who compose their own songs to bring the instrument they play or a tape of themselves singing.

Play each song (as loudly as possible without disturbing other classes). Encourage singing along. Invite the bringer to tell why he likes the song and invite others to add reasons they like the song. Close by pointing out that living the Christian life is not always easy. Music can be part of the encouragement we need.

CHARACTER THEME SONG

Guide youth to choose a tune from a commercial, a hymn tune, or a popular tune and change the words to become the theme song of a Bible character. Possible characters and passages include:

- Eve (Genesis 1:27; 2:20-25; 3:1–4:2);
- Enoch (Genesis 5:18-24; Hebrews 11:5-6);
- Deborah (Judges 4:4–5:15);
- Lazarus (Luke 16:19-31);
- Holy Spirit (Acts 2:1-4, 14-16);
- Peter (Luke 22:54-62; John 21:15-24; Acts 2–4);
- Priscilla and Aquila (Acts 18:18-28).

CREATE A COMMERCIAL

Commercial-writing is the perfect non-music-lover's entry to using music to study the Bible. Teenagers can compose brilliantly worded commercials that express Bible truth profoundly.
Commercial ideas include:

- Create a commercial that shows why Jesus' peace is superior to the peace the world offers (John 14).
- Write a commercial that shows how obeying God brings more freedom than living your own way (Romans 7:14–8:4).
- Sell chastity: Include why waiting until marriage makes sex better (Genesis 2:23-25, Hebrews 13:4, and Proverbs 5:15-20).

FIND A SONG

Let youth know what your next Bible study passage or theme is and invite them to bring songs that relate to it. These songs can be contemporary Christian music, hymns, or songs they have composed. (Be sure to arrange for a way to play the music.)

Use the songs as an introduction, to clarify a point, or as a closure.

The beauty of music is its ability to communicate and to help us remember. The beauty of this activity is that youth participate in the teaching.

ADAPTATION: If you didn't plan ahead, distribute hymnals when students arrive and challenge them to find a hymn on your theme.

HYMN EVALUATION

Guide youth to evaluate how closely their favorite hymns match the Bible. Many hymnals include Scripture indexes at the back. Some also print the passage on which each hymn is based at the bottom of the hymn page.

1. Bring the hymnal for each student or pair of students.

2. Direct them to find a hymn matching the passage/theme you are studying, or choose any hymn with a Bible reference.

3. Guide them to find in each stanza:

- A phrase they think agrees with the Scripture;
- A phrase that disagrees with Scripture or could be worded better;
- A way to reword the wrong or poorly worded phrase.

LISTENING SHEET

If you want students to listen closely to a song, distribute the lyrics with certain words missing and challenge your students to listen for and fill in the missing words. Choose the most important words to leave blank so youth will notice them.

MUSIC BIBLE STUDY

A music Bible study differs from "Bring a Song" because its goal is to evaluate music rather than to affirm one another's favorites. To hold a music Bible study, invite all your students to bring a currently popular song (secular or sacred) with the words written out on large paper. Explain that together you'll sing and evaluate these songs. Arrange for a way to play the songs. Bring several songs currently in the top 10 to supplement.

Play each song (as loudly as possible without disturbing other classes), encouraging all youth to sing along.

Invite students to find one phrase that agrees with something in the Bible and one phrase that disagrees. Point out that even music labeled "Christian" might teach things contrary to the Bible and music labeled "secular" might have Bible truth in it. Encourage youth to evaluate every song they hear, regardless of its label.

Continue evaluating by asking questions like these:

● What does this song teach about love? About life? About people? On what points is it right? Wrong?

● What is the song forgetting to tell us? (For example: sex outside marriage isn't free of complications.)

● If we did exactly as these words suggest, what would happen?

● What's encouraging about this song? Discouraging?

● How does this song encourage your Christian life? Frustrate its expression?

● What solutions does the song suggest? How do they work?

● What words do you like? What would you change?

Close by praising youth's insight and by encouraging them to evaluate everything they see and hear. Communicate your confidence in their ability to make smart choices.

VARIATION: Use this process to evaluate TV, magazines, books.

MUSIC VIDEO

Guiding students to make a music video takes time but is well worth it. Videos work especially well with "boring" passages because the procedure motivates interest. Youth dig deeply in their Bibles for facts to make their songs interesting.

Music videos also tie a series of lessons together well: students can write lyrics as their application step each week and then film the lyrics as a set at the end of the unit of study.

PERSONAL SONG

Assign each youth another youth to write a song for. Let the song be an affirmation of expressed faith, an encouragement to resist a temptation, or an expression of confidence in the ability to handle a challenge ahead.

Give time for students to interview those for whom they are writing (letting pairs write for each other makes this process easier). Encourage asking others for ideas. Make the experience positive.

VARIATION: Make singing telegrams, complete with actions.

WRITE A NEW VERSE TO A HYMN

Much of our understanding of God comes from the hymns we sing. Make your hymns even more meaningful by adding new verses based on Bible passages you're studying.

PLUS ...
Consider these other options for teaching your Bible passage:
- Sing a hymn or chorus that relates to your study.
- Speak a hymn (to focus on the words).
- Study the content of songs the choir will sing.
- Assemble a special choir to present a musical.
- Memorize songs or memorize Scripture to music.
- Play theme-related music as youth enter, do projects, leave.
- Study Bible instruments and song styles.

11
Learning Projects
Guide Youth to Present Their Learning to Others

Rationale: Possibly the most reliable indicator of learning is being able to present that learning to someone else. A project enables youth to do this. Projects provide triple learning:
1. Students learn while creating the project;
2. Students learn while presenting the project;
3. Students learn while watching others present their projects.

Students can create projects independently or in teams of two or more. When youth work together they build teamwork, experience success, feel part of a group, and become more comfortable going to the Bible for answers. The examples in this chapter work especially well for team projects.

Teaching Tip: Give specific and step-by-step instructions. The better students understand the process, the greater success they'll have. They will struggle less with "how" and can focus on "what."

CREATE A DATE
Provide paper, poster board, pipe cleaners, scissors, fake fur, markers and whatever else you have available. Direct youth to create the ideal date. Discuss with questions like, What makes him or her so attractive? So fun? How does this date love you as God loves you?

VARIATIONS: Create the ideal parent, best friend, or ultimate reject (then discuss ways to love the reject).

DEBATE
Debates help youth teach each other. They work well with issues that youth are defensive about because they enable youth to express

beliefs from an offensive position. They also work well with long-standing or unresolved issues because they help youth discover that faith can be complicated but can stand even with incomplete under-standing. Let youth search the Scriptures and draw their own conclu-sions with a brief informal debate. Follow these steps:

1. As students enter, direct them to draw slips of paper from an envelope. If it says PRO, they argue for the statement, no matter how they personally feel. If it says CON, they argue against the statement, no matter how they personally feel. Debating for some-thing they don't agree with forces youth to see both sides of the issue and deepens their convictions.

2. Post the debate statement. (For example, "Social drinking is acceptable.")

3. Offer to both PRO and CON sides Bible passages, resources about the issue, and other relevant information as applicable.

4. Allow two or three minutes of preparation time (too much time leads to distraction).

5. Call on the PRO team to speak for 90 seconds, each member speaking at least part of the time. Then call on the CON team to speak for 90 seconds, each member speaking. Encourage teams to take notes while the other team speaks.

6. Direct each team to prepare a rebuttal using the other's points and adding further evidence for their side.

7. Call on the CON side to present its rebuttal, followed by PRO.

8. Declare open season and all-out arguing. Supplement with points you want to make and by highlighting youth's wise statements.

FOLD-IN

Remember the feature on the back of every *Mad* magazine that folds in to reveal a truth? Guide youth to create similar fold-ins with both words and pictures. This is one procedure that youth consistently do better than their teachers. Use captions like these:

● Know what happens when you obey this command? Fold in to see.

● Fold in to see what happens when you ignore God's command to _____.

● How can you avoid this Bible character's mistake? Fold in to see.

● Fold on the dotted lines to see how you can find joy.

GAME CREATION

Chapter 5 details several learning games. Double game learning by guiding students to create the games themselves. Simpler games, like Bible Concentration, Bible Trivia, and Fact Match, can be created and played during the same session. More complex games or games with more questions may be created one week and played the next.

To create a game, follow these steps:

1. Decide the game format to be used or offer two options.

2. Decide what materials and content are needed for the game. For example, simplified Trivial Pursuit needs these materials: colored triangles to make a pie and a die covered with colored squares. It needs this content: several questions about the Bible passage.

3. Guide students to prepare the content. A team of four might divide the Bible passages into fourths and each write questions.

4. Instruct teams to prepare the materials. For simplified Trivial Pursuit, one cuts the squares for the die; one glues them; one cuts the triangles. One recopies questions so they're readable.

I.D. CARD

Write or guide youth to write cards that verify their identities as Christians or as those who live a particular command of God. Let the words of the card grow out of the passage you are studying. For example:

> I, _____, having accepted Jesus Christ, am now part of a _____ people, a royal _____, a _____ nation, a people belonging to _____. Because of this I will praise God, who called me out of darkness into His wonderful _____ (1 Peter 2:9).
>
> Signed: _____

VARIATION: Write certificates of adoption into God's family.

INTERVIEW

Send pairs of students out to people in your church to interview them on the theme or passage you are studying. Arrange the interview ahead so you will not interrupt a class or meeting. A few questions asked of several people usually works better than one long list of questions for one person. Possibilities:

● Interview heads of church committees on what their committees do.

● Ask a preschooler, child, youth, young adult, median adult, and senior adult to tell what God means to them. Compare and contrast.

● Ask several people how they pray, forgive, or do another faith action you are studying.

VARIATION: Collect questions about God and then invite the pastor or a staff minister to come answer them. Let youth discover that even pastors still search.

VARIATION: Take a tape recorder while interviewing.

VARIATION: Interview other youth (requires no prearrangement).

JOB DESCRIPTION

Juniors and seniors who have filled out job applications or are deciding on a career will like this activity. Guide them to write a job description based on the passage you are studying. Possibilities include:

● Develop a job description for a "Christian at _____ High School" based on Colossians 3.

● Write a job description for the Holy Spirit based on Acts 2:1-4 and John 14–16.

● Write a job descrition for a close relationship with God based on 2 Chronicles 7:14-16.

LEARNING CENTERS

Learning centers are self-contained learning experiences that allow youth to choose what they will learn and how. They are especially valuable for studying Bible passages that are very familiar; students almost always discover something new.

To prepare learning centers you need:

● Instruction sheets to place at each center;

● Materials to complete the instructions;

● You to circulate and encourage.

Arrange the centers around the room, some on tables, some on the floor depending on the nature of the learning experience. Demonstrate how to complete a learning center by holding up an instruction sheet, reading it, and following the instructions. Point out the learning centers. Encourage students to complete as many centers as they can during the hour.

Call everyone back to a large circle 10 minutes before the session is over. Share discoveries with such questions as: What did you learn that you didn't know before? What was your favorite center and why?

Who would like to show something you created at a center?

ADAPTATION: Guide youth to create and present learning centers. These Christmas learning centers may give you ideas for creating your own.

• Center 1: Order the Facts

Instructions: Next to this instruction sheet is a stack of eight cards. Each card lists an event that occurred during the first Christmas. Place these in order according to Luke 1:26-38 and Matthew 1:18-25. Then check yourself by looking at the penciled numbers on the back. (No cheating by looking early!) When you finish, scramble the cards and display them for the next person.

Materials: Bibles. Facts one to a card, numbered in order in pencil on the back.

1. Gabriel visited Mary.
2. Mary was troubled.
3. Mary asked how she, a virgin, could have a baby.
4. The angel explained that God would be the Father of the baby.
5. Mary agreed to be Jesus' mother.
6. Joseph planned to quietly break off the engagement when he found out Mary was pregnant.
7. Joseph had a dream.
8. Joseph married Mary and waited until after Jesus' birth to have sex with her.

• Center 2: Concentration Game

Instructions: Prepare a "concentration game" on the first Christmas. You will need a Bible, eight index cards, and a marker.

1. Choose four facts from the Christmas story. You may use Matthew 1:18-25 or Matthew 2:1-13.
2. Write half the fact on one card and half on the other. Or you can write the person who said it on one card and a quote on the other. Write the Bible reference on one card so answers can be checked.
3. Find someone to play your game.

Materials: Several sets of eight cards, markers, Bibles.

• Center 3: What's the Password?

Instructions: Find three other people. Sit in two rows, facing each other. The person across from you is your partner. The two of you will help each other guess words from Isaiah 7:14 and 9:6.

1. Set the password cards upside down on the floor between you.
2. All four of you open your Bibles to Isaiah 9:6 and put your fingers in Isaiah 7:14 so you can flip back and forth.
3. Decide who will go first. That person draws a password card and gives a one-word clue to the partner. If the partner guesses right, award 10 points. If not, the other team gets a chance to give a clue. Go back and forth until the word is guessed or the points are zero.
4. Move on to the next word, alternating who goes first. Keep your eyes on the Bible verses to help you guess the words. (NOTE: if your translations vary, the word in your Bible is the right one.)
5. Shuffle the cards after you finish for the next group.

Materials: Paper to keep score, pencil, Bibles, four chairs facing each other, set of shuffled cards with these words, one to a card: SIGN, VIRGIN, SON, IMMANUEL, US, WONDERFUL, COUNSELOR, MIGHTY, GOD, PRINCE, PEACE.

● **Center 4: I Was There**
Instructions: Choose to be one of the characters at the birth of Jesus Christ (yes, donkeys and sheep included). Write what you see, feel, hear, smell, taste, and think about this. You can also write your experiences in cartoon form.
Materials: Bibles, paper, and pencils.

● **Center 5: Sing a Song of Christmas**
Instructions: Read Luke 1:26–2:20, writing down facts that impress you. Choose a familiar Christmas carol and write a new verse using the ideas you wrote down. Post your song on the wall when you finish.
Materials: Bibles, paper, pencils, hymnals or Christmas carol books.

● **Center 6: Create a Crossword Puzzle**
Instructions: Read John 1:1-18, which tells the Christmas story from a different perspective. Underline key words such as "Word," "beginning," and "light." Create a crossword puzzle with these words, using clues from the Scripture passage. Use the graph paper provided to write the words. Then copy it over with blank squares. Find someone to solve your crossword puzzle.
Materials: Bibles, graph paper, pencils with erasers.

MANUAL FOR CHRISTIAN LIVING

Guide youth to work in teams, or as a single group if your class is small, to create a manual with do's, don'ts, and how's on a topic like these:

● Dating manual written by guys for girls;
● Dating manual written by girls for guys;
● Witnessing manual containing "do's," "don'ts," what to say;
● How to travel the "Roman road" to salvation using Romans 3:23; 5:8; 6:23; 10:9-10; 12:1-2;
● How to live the Christian life at school;
● Prayer manual with pages on praise, petition, intercession, confession;
● How to keep cool in the middle of an argument;
● Guide for family happiness.

Encourage youth to construct their manuals according to the specific Bible passages you are studying. (For more ideas, see "Evangelism and Witnessing Booklet" in chapter 13.)

MARKED BIBLE

Challenge youth to mark a Bible to give guidance on assignments like those under "Manual for Christian Living." Provide topical Bibles and plenty of ideas. A marked Bible begins with "Turn to page _____" on the inside cover. At each location, underline or highlight the verse and put "Turn to page _____" for the next entry. For the last page, encourage students to write something like: "Now you have lots of ideas for creating a great date!"

MAZE CREATION
Guide youth to create mazes that lead through theme words and actions for your passage. Wrong turns lead through words that don't match the passage or through the results of not obeying it.

NEWSPAPER
Newspapers can be simple or quite complex. To complete one in a single session, cut apart a large piece of paper and reassemble it after youth have completed their assignments: one piece becomes article space, one becomes illustration space, one becomes cartoon space, one becomes advice letters, one becomes a crossword puzzle or jumble puzzle, one becomes want ads, and so on.

Because newspapers contain so many different elements, they allow youth to learn in several different ways (word-learners choose articles, art-learners choose comics, feeling-learners choose advice columns, and so on). Let youth choose the element they want to work on.

VARIATION: Guide youth to write headlines for Bible passages.

PERSONAL INVENTORY
Are you a shopaholic? How dateable are you? What's your friendship IQ? Youth turn to these features first in magazines and newspapers. Their desire for self-understanding makes personal inventories a great teaching tool. Guide youth to create inventories on topics like:
- Do you love as Jesus loves?
- How committed are you to Christ?
- How well do you show your faith in daily life?

To create personal inventories:

1. Choose a topic that matches your Bible passage.

2. Guide youth to create at least 10 questions, each with three responses, such as "S=seldom," "U=usually," "M=most of the time."

3. Let the questions come directly from your Bible passage. Sample questions from Ephesians 4:17-32 might include:

I am sensitive to the needs of others (v. 19)	S	U	M
I replace negative desires with positive ones (22)	S	U	M
I use caring words rather than cutting ones (29)	S	U	M

4. Add scoring instructions like these: For every "seldom" give yourself 1 point; For every "usually" give yourself 2 points; For every "most of the time" give yourself 3 points.

    1-10 points = A Sunday-only Christian

    11-15 points = growing

    16-20 points = you're starting to notice that God's ways work

    21-25 points = experiencing the peace that passes understanding

    26-30 points = full-blown joy

5. Trade inventories and score yourselves. Discuss with: What was your biggest surprise? What are you proud of? What will you change?

TELEVISION OR RADIO SHOW

Guide youth to use the format of a favorite TV or radio show to present Bible information. Standards which tend to work are guest interviews, talk shows, news programs, or dramatic radio readings. Possibilities:

• Hold a top 10 radio countdown with the 10 facts you find most important in today's passage.

• Invite Joseph's brothers to visit your talk show and answer questions from the audience on getting along with siblings.

• Sing or read Mary's song and Zechariah's from Luke 1:46-55; 67-79.

WORD STUDY

Bible words *("suffer* the little children to come unto me") and illustrations can be hard to understand because our words and life experiences are different. Other Bible words are packed with theological meaning (like *justification* and *sanctification).* Guide youth to define and study these words with such tools as other translations, Bible dictionaries, and Bible concordances. Samples:

• Direct youth to read a verse with confusing words in several translations. For example: "Suffer the little children" in the King James Version of Matthew 19:14 reads "Let the little children" in the New International Version.

• Direct youth to look up the words in a readable Bible dictionary (or in the commentary of your curriculum). Choose a dictionary brief enough to be clear, but long enough to give adequate detail.

● Guide youth to use a Bible concordance to read the word in other verses where it is used.

After youth have studied words and phrases, direct them to write definitions in memorable form. Perhaps they'll write the word on one card and the definition on another card, shuffle them, display them face down, and play "Bible Concentration" (see chapter 5 for details). Maybe they'll shape "sanctification" with a lump of clay saying, "Sanctification is letting God mold me into a happy person."

WORSHIP SERVICE

This project involves every youth in preparing, leading, and partici-pating in worship. As students enter, assign them to one of the following groups (or let them choose). If your class is small, let one person be a team or reduce the number of elements your service has. Spend the first three-fourths of class preparing in teams for the worship experience and the last fourth experiencing worship. Call on teams to present their portion of worship in order: Song, Scripture reading, Praise, Sermon, Prayer.

Circulate and guide teams as they work, encouraging them to complete their project step-by-step. Substitute your own themes and passages.

● **Song Team:** Write an opening song for our worship experience using a familiar tune. Let your song express praise and adoration to Jesus Christ.

● **Scripture Reading Team:** Choose phrases from Revelation 4:1–8:5 that praise and honor God. Write them in your own words or put the verse in the order you like, then assign each verse to a group. (Example: Boys read odd verses; girls read even verses; all read the final verse.)

● **Praise Team:** Make a poster or banner that symbolizes thanks-giving, praise, and adoration of Christ. After explaining your creation, invite the group to name things they praise Jesus for.

● **Sermon Team:** Prepare a sermon (three minutes maximum) based on Revelation 4:1–8:5 for our worship experience. Include these three points:

1. Talk about worshiping idols today. Name some we worship.

2. Tell why these idols are easy to worship but are not worthy of worship.

3. Tell why Christ is worthy of worship.

● **Prayer Team:** Write a closing prayer for our worship experience. Using your own words, express ideas from Revelation 4:1–8:5. Write your prayer on large paper so we can all read it together.

PLUS...
Consider these other options for teaching your Bible passage:
- Mission trip to learn about missions (start in your own community);
- Slide show about the passage;
- Book report;
- Programmed learning (answer questions and immediately see answers);
- T-shirt iron-on that communicates the truth you study;
- Notebook or journal of a multi-session study;
- Music video.

12
Bible Memory Joggers
Remember Tomorrow What You Studied Today

Rationale: "I have hidden Your Word in my heart that I might not sin against You" (Psalm 119:11).

My students say they can't memorize.

We try Scripture memory, but the kids say it's boring.

Bible memory doesn't have to be hard or boring. Teenagers memorize every day. They memorize the words to songs on the radio, telephone numbers of friends, answers to the next test, and more. Use these skills to memorize the Bible.

Teaching Tip: After each Bible memory experience, help youth understand it by asking, "How did this help you memorize the verse? How will you live what you memorized?"

ACCOUNTABILITY

Pair youth so they can quiz each other on memorized verses. Have them exchange phone numbers and call each other at midweek and recite for each other. Take time during class to check each other.

ACROSTIC

Challenge youth to organize the Bible verse in phrases so it spells a word. This example uses a nonsense word: HAT-LAM.

"He has showed you, O man, what is good.

And what does the Lord require of you?

To act justly and to

Love mercy

And to walk humbly with your God."

Micah 6:8

CARD BY CARD

Write each word of the passage on a separate card. For long passages, write phrases or entire verses on the cards. Use the cards for:

* **Unscramble:** Shuffle the cards and challenge youth to place them in the correct order, looking at their Bibles for verification. Repeat, encouraging youth to beat their previous times.
* **Elimination:** Once the cards are in order, direct students to repeat the verse a couple times. Then remove a key word and challenge youth to repeat the verse filling in the word. Continue repeating and removing words until the verse is memorized.
* **Human Scramble:** Give one card to each youth. Give them 60 seconds to arrange themselves in correct order. Congratulate them, collect and shuffle the cards, redistribute them, and challenge youth to do it in less time than before. HINT: Youth may stand exactly backward, forgetting the perspective of the reader. If this happens, laugh along and give 15 more seconds.

CREDIT CARD

Explain that God's Word is valuable and a reminder of it deserves to be kept with our other valuables. Distribute credit-card-sized papers (white poster board works well) and markers, and guide youth to write out and illustrate the memory verse(s). Explain: You can count on the truth in this passage more than you count on a credit card. Keep your "credit" in your billfold or wallet to remind you to use it.

HINT: This idea is especially appropriate for Bible promises.

MEMORY BY RHYTHM

Guide youth to memorize Bible verses or truths by setting them to a rhythm, rap pattern, self-composed music, or favorite song tune. Repeatedly sing the rhythm as a group and then gradually add the words to the tune. Repeat until the words fit the rhythm.

NOTE: This is an excellent way for a youth who may be new to the Bible and to church to participate. If he has musical talent, invite him to start the rhythm or rap and the rest to sing along. This youth is the leader in a familiar area and becomes open to the Bible.

MISSING LETTERS

Write the verse on a poster or individual cards but leave out key words or letters. You might all remove all vowels, as in the Hebrew language. Challenge youth to fill in the missing parts.

VARIATION: Scramble the words or letters within words. Challenge youth to unscramble them.

PERSONAL MEMORY

Good naturedly explain that, though it's seldom easy to memorize an entire verse, memorizing one or two words is easy. Assign to each youth one word or phrase from the verse you want to memorize. Direct them to recite their words in order, each youth standing in turn. Do this several times and then challenge volunteers to recite as much of the passage as they can by looking at each classmate and saying his or her word. Point out that they memorized the entire verse by hearing each other say the words.

A PICTURE IS WORTH A THOUSAND WORDS

Invite students to doodle or draw a single picture of the Bible verse. Then instruct them to recite the verse using the clues in the picture. For example, Psalm 119:11 ("I have hidden Your Word in my heart that I might not sin against You") might be a large heart with "Word" hiding in one of the folds and a sign with "sin" crossed out.

POPULAR TUNES

Guide youth to choose a tune they like and sing a Bible verse to it. These tunes can be commercial jingles, hymns, or contemporary songs. Write the original words syllable-by-syllable and substitute the Bible verse words. Sing as a group repeatedly until it is memorized.

PUZZLE CUBES

Memorize several related verses at once by writing one fourth of each verse on a card and taping the card to different sides of four blocks. Youth arrange the blocks with the correct side up in proper order. Seeing the verse segments during arranging helps them memorize the verses.

REBUS

A rebus is a combination of words and pictures that form a phrase. For example, the word "for" might literally be drawn "4." The word "near" might be indicated by "n" followed by a picture of an ear. Words like "the" might be left as is

When students write their own rebuses, the time they spend concentrating on the words helps them memorize the verse. To build confidence the first few times you try this activity, you might distribute the verse with blanks already in place for words that would be easy to illustrate.

RECORDED SCRIPTURE
Many Bible verses have been recorded word-for-word by Christian artists. The Bible translation varies from artist to artist. One example is "Psalm 95" on the album *Come to the Quiet* by John Michael Talbot (Sparrow Records). The tune helps teens remember the verses.

SCHOOL CHEER
Guide youth to develop a cheer or cheers based on the verse(s) to be memorized. Ideally cheers should repeat the verse word-for-word, but you can allow rephrasing when the meaning remains the same. The best process is to choose a school cheer, write it with a blank line after each phrase, and then write the Bible verse on the blank lines, matching the cheer syllable-for-syllable.

TEACHING TAPE
Guide youth to make their own teaching tape imitating the language teaching tapes. Let them take turns saying each phrase of the Bible verse into a tape recorder. After each phrase is spoken, leave a blank space on the tape long enough to repeat that phrase. Finally record the entire verse in unison and allow enough space to repeat it.

Play the tape back and invite the entire group to repeat each phrase during the blank segments. Duplicate one copy of the tape for every youth. They can then play the tape while in the car or while dressing.

ADAPTATION: If you have a large group, guide them to work in teams to record different verses. Then exchange tapes.

TRANSLATION COMPARISON
Invite youth to read the memory verse from several translations (the Bibles students bring usually provide variety). Ask volunteers to share the wording they like best. Continue with questions such as: Which words really bring out the meaning of this verse?

As you talk about different translations, remind youth that the original Bible was written in Hebrew and Greek, so we all read from translations. Reading from several translations is one of the best ways to understand the meaning of a verse, and thus to remember it.

PLUS...

These ideas, discussed in detail in other chapters, are also excellent Bible memory methods:

- Bible Concentration (chapter 5);
- Crossword Grid (chapter 7);
- Decode the Truth (chapter 7);
- Guess the Word (chapter 5);
- Letter Board (chapter 5);
- Mazes (chapter 7);
- Telephone Number (chapter 7);
- Trading Game (chapter 5; use for verses with lists such as the fruit of the spirit, spiritual gifts, brothers of Joseph, more).

13
Life Application
Experience Can Be the Best Teacher

Rationale: Jesus taught frequently through experience. The Samaritan woman experienced God's acceptance through Jesus (John 4:1-26). The 12 Apostles learned about ministry by ministering according to Jesus' instructions (Mark 6:7-13). The woman caught in adultery experienced forgiveness from Jesus and perhaps from many who walked away without stoning her (John 8:3-11). Peter, James, and John experienced a taste of heaven at the Transfiguration (Mark 9:2-13). We teachers can provide similar life-changing experiences in Bible study.

Teaching Tip: Notice your youth's specific needs and questions and create Bible study experiences to meet those needs and answer those questions. Whenever possible let at least one student help you write or set up the learning experience. This makes them truer to life and involves that student in learning through preparing.

AFFIRMATION
Guide students to give and experience acceptance through affirmation. Direct each youth to write his or her name vertically on paper. Instruct them to pass their papers to the left and to write a Christlike characteristic that starts with one letter of the name. Pass the name page five times. If a name runs out of letters, use a letter again. Call for the person holding the card after five passes to introduce the person on the card by reading the compliments. Return the cards to original owners so they can keep them as an affirmation of Christ in them and encouragement to keep Him shining. Ask: How does it feel to have your friends notice good in you?

VARIATION: While studying the name of Jesus, point out that the name meant the person. Ask: What characteristics spell Jesus? How do our characteristics make us who we are? What else do you want to spell?

VARIATION: Let youth fill out their own name to encourage them to live their faith. Their name will remind them of the qualities. Samples:

- A way I can live my faith, using each letter of my name;
- A way I can live _____ (the passage you're studying);
- How I am a part of the body of Christ (1 Corinthians 12:12-13).

VARIATION: On the first Sunday of a new year, let students introduce each other to you via name affirmation.

DILEMMAS

Whenever you study a Bible passage that demonstrates God's problem-solving strategies, invite youth to submit dilemmas they face (anonymously if they prefer). Apply the Bible strategies to solving the dilemmas.

When discussing dilemmas, show that there are frequently more than two options. The familiar story tells of a hand grenade in the room. Youth may feel they have two options: (1) to throw themselves on the grenade to save their friends or (2) to let the grenade go off and kill everyone. Guide them to see a third option: throwing the hand grenade out the window.

VARIATION: Use case studies—pre-written dilemmas in another's life.

EMPATHY THROUGH MULTIPLE CHOICE SHARING

Promote empathy (feeling with the other) and the realization that we all have similar experiences by inviting youth to compare themselves to a Bible character or experience. Each question or sentence fragment is followed by several options, plus a blank line if youth prefer to write their own response. This sample examines Cain and Abel (Genesis 4:1-16):

1. I'm like Cain because:
   a. I'm the oldest child in my family.
   b. I neglect to bring my best to God.
   c. I feel like killing my brother/sister.
   d. I act nice when I have evil intentions.
   e. _____

2. I'm like Abel because:
   a. I'm a younger child in my family.
   b. I bring my best to God.
   c. I have been attacked by my brother/sister.
   d. I don't always notice evil intentions.
   e. _____

3. After I've done wrong like Cain I:
   a. Avoid God's questions.
   b. Avoid God.
   c. Try to get away with what I have done.
   d. Complain that life is not fair.
   e. _____

4. When God and I talk about sin I:
   a. Try to talk Him out of punishing me (v. 13).
   b. Find myself amazed that He still cares (v. 15).
   c. Move away from the people I have hurt (v. 16).
   d. Move away from God (v. 16).
   e. _____

5. A sin I have let build is:
   a. jealousy, which led to revenge, which led to the end of a relationship.
   b. lying, which led to more lying and covering up.
   c. deception, which led to hurting someone, which led to denying it.
   d. avoiding God, which led to feeling distant from Him.
   e. _____

EVANGELISM AND WITNESSING BOOKLET

Guide youth to become equipped for witnessing by preparing their own guides to becoming a Christian. Let them grow out of the evangelistic passage(s) you are studying. A simple version is a piece of paper folded in half and numbered in four pages. Sample:

- **Cover page:** Create a cover with a symbol of new life in Christ.
- **Inside page 1:** List steps to becoming a Christian.
- **Inside page 2:** Write a prayer or prayers someone could pray to become a Christian. Include tips for praying.
- **Back page:** Give examples of things new Christians do and don't do. Make the DO list longer than the DON'T list. (Christians DO enjoy friends that really care; Christians DON'T spend much time with friends that discourage or tempt them.)

To use the above booklet or witness in other ways, guide youth to create a "Witnessing Booklet." Use instructions like these:

- **Cover page:** Create a cover including a symbol for witnessing or questions the booklet answers.
- **Inside page 1:** Suggest Scriptures to use to lead someone to become a Christian. Include how to explain the verses.

- **Inside page 2:** Give DO's and DON'Ts for witnessing. Sample: DO act natural. DON'T act holier-than-thou.
- **Back page:** List excuses people give for not witnessing and ways to overcome each excuse.

Consider publishing both booklets for the church.

INVITATION TO BECOME A CHRISTIAN

The most important real-life experience is to accept Jesus Christ as Saviour and Lord. Regularly offer an invitation during your Bible study. Let invitations grow out of the passages you are studying. Sample ways:

- When studying John 3:1-16 or another evangelistic passage, include all youth in a time of decision with a multiple choice card:

_____ I want to become a Christian.

_____ I want to become a Christian but I have questions.

_____ I have become a Christian and want to obey Christ by _____.

_____ I _____.

Invite volunteers to share decisions publically.

- Invite youth to share ways they are growing in Christ. Ask: How is Christianity a series of decisions rather than just one?
- Pass out a guide that tells in steps how to become a Christian. Assign each youth a step and direct them to explain it to the class.
- Guide youth to talk with God about salvation with sentence starters like these:

God, when I think of Jesus dying for me . . .

Sins I want to confess to You include . . .

God, knowing You love me even though I've done wrong . . .

God, I accept Your love, Your forgiveness, Your salvation. Please guide my life starting with . . .

I'm so glad to be a part of Your family because . . .

I want my life to be different by . . .

- Invite youth to give 10- to 30-second testimonies on why they are Christians or would like to become Christians. Lead a time of private prayer inviting any who have not become Christians to do so.
- Use quality tracts and invite youth to explain them to each other.

Close with delight over those who have accepted Jesus during this hour. Encourage them to make their decision public during the next church worship service. Offer to go with them when they do so. Encourage all to live their commitment to Christ, whether made now or in the past.

LIFE MOTTO
Guide youth to declare a life motto based upon the truth you are studying. Samples:

- Ephesians 4:29: "Compliments, not cuts" — OR — "Use loving words, not sarcasm."
- 1 Thessalonians 5:17: "Jesus is my steering wheel, not a spare tire."
- Psalm 23: "God will get me through anything."

MULTIPLE ENDINGS
When discussing ethical issues, guide pairs of youth to write a story with multiple endings, similar to the "choose your own mystery" books. This extra creative procedure may take most of the Bible study time, but guides youth to experience decision-making and consequences of those decisions. Suggest that each ending be the result of a certain choice. Deuteronomy 30:19-20 goes well with this procedure.

PRETEND YOU ARE THERE
Guide youth to prepare for real-life circumstances or experience what Bible characters experienced by pretending they are in the circumstance you name. They may focus better if they close their eyes. Possibilities:

- Pretend you are in the room praying when Peter comes to say he has been set free. What are you thinking? Feeling? Doing? What do you say to Peter? (Acts 12:13-17)
- Pretend you have just died. Where are you going now? What does heaven look like? What does Jesus say to you when you meet Him? What do you say to Him? What questions do you ask Him? How do you feel? (John 14:1-3; Revelation 21)
- Pretend you have just died. What are people saying about you? What do they miss about you? How did you impact their lives? Open your eyes and rewrite your own obituary/epitaph. (Scripture options include Ephesians 5:15 and Colossians 3:1-17.)
- Pretend you are riding in a car with your best friend. Another car runs a red light and smashes into yours. When you come to, you realize your friend is not moving. You feel for a pulse, there is none. How do you live the truths in Philippians 4:13, 19 or 1 Thessalonians 4:13-18?
- Pretend the day you have been looking for has arrived. Jesus

has returned. What are you doing when He comes? What does He say and do? What else is going on? (Read Mark 13 for ideas.)

• Pretend your house is on fire. The people are out safely and you have time to save three items. What will they be and why?

SENSORY LEARNING

Think of ways to use all five senses as youth learn. Some studies show that smell produces the longest memory. Let these possibilities give you more ideas:

• **Smell:** Noah's ark; the sweet savor of prayer; Lazarus' death; Jonah in the fish;

• **Taste:** Figs; loaves and fishes; salt of the earth; milk; meat;

• **Hear:** Scripture set to music; other's insights on Scripture; sound track;

• **See:** Posters; cartoons; photographs; video; eyes;

• **Feel:** Fellowship hugs; crown of thorns; weight of burdens;

SET-UPS

Set up a situation before youth enter to help them experience the theme. Possibilities include:

• Leave a plate of cookies on an unsupervised table with a sign that says, "Do not eat." Follow with a study on temptation.

• Lay a youth volunteer on the table and cover her with a sheet. As the other youth enter ask: Is this person dead? How can you tell? The person may begin to giggle when others poke at her. Point out that, though she may pretend to be dead, she cannot be dead unless she really is. What qualities would she need to be dead? How do you know the person is alive? Follow by studying spiritual life and death. Use passages like Romans 6:1-8.

• Invite a friend to pose as a new youth who is very shy or dresses differently. Notice the way youth relate to him. Follow with a study on Luke 14:1-14 or another passage on acceptance and love.

• Pack everyone into a small room without a window. Turn out the lights and study passages like 1 John 1–2 (living in the light), John 11:1-44 (Lazarus raised from death), Acts 12:1-11 (Peter's escape from prison), and passages detailing Paul's imprisonments.

VIDEO CREATION

Creating and watching a video takes considerable time, but the effects can be life changing. Types include:

- **Training video:** Prepare a series of role plays which show right and wrong ways to witness, make friends, comfort someone during crisis, or whatever your theme. Base it on Scripture.
- **Retreat video:** If your Bible study takes place at a retreat, lock-in, or camp, guide youth to video selected discussions, simulations, testimonies (with permission, of course).
- **Charade Bible memory verses:** Make certain verses memorable by acting them out phrase by phrase and filming them.
- **Music video:** Set Scripture points to music (see chapter 10).

WRITE YOUR OWN ENDING
Direct youth to write a new ending to a Bible passage or to a story. Let the story be an opportunity to benefit from the Bible character's mistake without having to make it. (For example, what if David had resisted sleeping with Bathsheba?) Be sure to compare the character's situation to decisions youth face today.

PLUS ...
Consider these other options for teaching your Bible passage:
- Simulations of other cultures;
- Mission trips to experience and grow through ministry to others;
- Real-life loving (send cards; call; invite; include; witness);
- Trust walk: one is blindfolded and the other leads;
- Write a will telling what you'll leave to whom and why;
- Write a will naming non-material things you'll leave to whom and why;
- A Quaker Meeting: silent until someone feels led to speak;
- Mock trial: "If you were arrested for Christianity (or a specific element of it) would there be enough evidence to convict you?";
- Testimonies (frequent and focused to increase comfort talking about Christ);
- Litany of praise.

14
Work the Bugs
Out of Your Teaching

Teaching Gets Better with Practice, Understanding, Training

Q: *My students are good kids; why can't I just sit them down and tell them about the Bible and how to live it? I can fit more Bible study in if we don't take time for all this arty and fun stuff.*

A: Just telling kids about the Bible may seem efficient, but it's quite easy for students to let your telling go in one ear and out the other. Youth can smile and be "good" but not learn a thing. The more involved they are in the Bible, the more they'll remember about it and the more they'll live what they learned. You can "fit more Bible study in" when you talk because you're summarizing the results of hours of your Bible study. Recall the mountain climbing illustration at the end of chapter 1: Would it be better to tell students about your climb or take them to the top of the mountain with you? Taking them to the top would take more time than saying, "The results are worth the climb." But which would change their lives? Guide youth to experience the exhilaration of discovering God's truth in the Bible, the joy of realizing that God's ways really are worth the effort.

Q: *I agree that youth need to study the Bible for themselves, but mine just aren't motivated. Why bother trying if they don't want to learn?*

A: Because the Bible has the answers they're looking for. Your students may not seem interested in the Bible, but they become interested when they discover the Bible has solutions to their problems and answers to their questions; "But whoever believes in Him will not be disappointed" (Romans 9:33, GNB). You guide youth to begin or deepen their spirituality when you motivate them to study the Bible. Motivation is:

- noticing youth's needs;
- addressing the needs you notice;
- showing how the Bible meets those needs.

Remember four elements of good motivation with these four M's:

	Meaningful;
	Moves toward the Bible;
involves	Movement;
uses the	Mouth.

Guide your youth toward meaningful Bible study by relating it to their lives. Show youth how moving toward the Bible answers their questions and gives them the happiness they seek. Youth learn better when some part of them is moving—especially on a sleepy Sunday morning or in an evening Bible study after a long day in school. Finally, because youth remember what they themselves say, encourage them to use their mouths.

Q: *If I do all this fancy stuff I won't have time for the Bible study. How can I fit it all in?*

A: The "fancy" stuff *is* the Bible study. Notice that a good Bible activity gets teenagers looking at and learning from their Bibles. For instance, Bible tic-tac-toe may seem like a mere game, but during it youth must search their Bibles for answers. During these repeated readings they learn Bible facts.

Recall that a good Bible teaching method doesn't entertain youth; it guides them to discover Bible answers for themselves. Entertaining youth can be just as boring and meaningless as lecturing to them.

Q: *I try to get my students to talk by asking questions, but they just sit there or one person answers all the questions. What can I do?*

A: Because it's risky to answer questions, many youth won't venture it. Make it safe by using methods that require everyone to speak. When everyone talks, no one feels "on the spot." Possibilities include:

- "Under-Chair Questions" (chapter 6);
- "Talk Around the Circle" (chapter 6);
- "Bible Jeopardy" (chapter 5);

• "Hot Bag" (chapter 6).

Second, when possible, choose subjects that youth are already interested in, like family relationships, friendship, dating, and problem-solving. Move the conversation to what the Bible says about the topic.

Third, try talk-motivators from chapter 8 such as: "Competition" (list more than the other team); "Prove Me Wrong" (prove this falsehood wrong); "Predicament Cubes" (solve the situation you roll with the attitude someone else rolls), "Agree/Disagree" (walking discussion).

Q: *My students talk just fine until I ask a question about the Bible. Then no one will say a word and I end up doing all the talking. Why won't my students talk about the Bible?*

A: Talking about boyfriends and ball games is easy because youth have had lots of practice. Make talking about the Bible just as easy by giving them practice at it. As they practice, help them feel safe and smart:

• Help students venture talking by valuing every contribution and by refusing to put anyone down for any answer, even if it's totally wrong. "Thank you for your idea. You thought hard!" is a positive response for a totally wrong answer. "You've got part of it. Keep looking!" is good for accurate or partly accurate responses. As youth's words are valued, they feel valued, and they talk more. Your valuing them eases their fear of looking dumb if they answer wrong.

• Youth need to know that what they say in class will make sense to others and that nobody will make fun of them for talking. Help this happen by forbidding any cutting. "In this class we listen to each other and value each other. I will not allow cuts or sarcasm."

• Increase youth's chance of answering factual questions correctly by giving an answer source. Take your questions directly from the Bible or student book so your students can find the answer by reading the assigned Bible verses or book section. When teens answer correctly, they gain confidence in reading and understanding the Bible.

• If someone struggles with a question, show her where to find the answer rather than calling on someone else. Let her redeem herself.

• When students answer incorrectly, point out the part of the answer that was right. "Paul was not one of the original 12 disciples, but he was a disciple in the way every Christian is a disciple."

Put yourself in the shoes of your students. What would make you more comfortable studying a subject you are only vaguely familiar with? What would motivate you to want to understand it better? Do that.

Q: *I passed out clay and asked my students to shape forgiveness. They just looked at me and said, "You've got to be kidding! We aren't children anymore. Why do we have to do this dumb stuff?"*

A: Youth worry intensely about looking dumb in front of their friends. The key to overcoming this worry often lies with your enthusiasm. Begin with, "Forgiveness is such a difficult concept to grasp that I want you to help me by making a symbol that represents it from this clay . . . " rather than, "Before we get to the heavy stuff let's play with clay for a while. . . ." If your group still resists, say something like, "Humor me and try it. Your ideas always impress me and I look forward to hearing them." Most youth enjoy what the teacher enjoys. In fact, high school seniors tend to enjoy clay shaping the most.

Q: *No matter what I do, my teenagers just won't quit talking. They have to share their romance stories, details about the ball games, and more.*

A: See these distractions as opportunities. Few youth come to Bible study sessions ready to focus on the Bible passage of the day. Rather than scolding your youth for this, recall your own thoughts as you walk into worship. All of us must move from current thoughts and worries to focus on God and His solutions to those thoughts and worries. Create Bible study sessions that invite youth to discover God's answers to the needs they feel. For example, when the lesson is on God's wrath and your students are intent on discussing a rumor at school, use the rumor to show how God's wrath works. Point out that God's wrath is letting us have the consequences of our actions. Ask, "What are some consequences in this case? What are issues? (gossip, revenge, pride) What does God advise? How are people deciding to respond to this advice? Who will be hurt or helped by these choices? Why would God's advice work?"

Move your students from what they're already talking about to what the Bible says about it. Help them see that the Bible holds the answers.

Q: *Again and again this book suggests leaving the Bible open during quizzes and games and other Bible learning activities. My students get all the answers right that way. If the kids are always looking in their Bibles, when are they going to learn the stuff on their own?*

A: When they leave class. We're not in Bible study to test youth's knowledge of the Bible but to give them opportunity to study it, understand it, and succeed with it so they'll trust the Bible for everyday guidance. The hour you teach guides youth to discover Bible answers they can use during life. Keep kids' noses in the Bibles for these reasons:

• The Bible is the source of answers. We want youth to have lots of experience noticing that.

• The more success youth have with getting Bible answers right, the more confident they'll feel about their own Bible skills and the more they'll read the Bible outside of class.

• We're in Bible study to teach youth the Bible, not to prove them wrong. Youth get plenty of experience with failure outside church; they don't need to cope with massive doses of it at church too.

• When youth do fail, point out the answer so they can see that the Bible will help them redeem mistakes too.

Q: *Why go to all the trouble to create a learning game? Why not just ask the questions in discussion format?*

A: It does seem more trouble, but the trouble is worth it because:

• In discussions, one or two people tend to answer all the questions. Learning games invite participation from the entire group.

• Learning games give shyer kids a chance to talk and non-"school-smart" kids a chance to shine by doing the game skillfully.

• Moving encourages attention. Youth are frequently tired on Sunday mornings. If their bodies are moving, their brains can't go to sleep.

• The game itself catches their attention and motivates youth to dig in their Bibles. Some youth will be there because their parents made them come. They have little, if any, interest in spiritual things. They will have interest in the game, however, as they play, they'll discover that the Bible has the answers they've been looking for.

Learning games can be as simple as drawing a tic-tac-toe board on the chalkboard or arranging chairs in three rows of three. They don't have to be complex, but they are almost always effective.

Q: *My students never bring their Bibles. How can we do Bible study without Bibles?*

A: It's almost a rite of passage that youth in seventh grade stop bringing Bibles. To encourage them to bring their own Bibles:
- Use them frequently. Kids tend to bring what they need.
- Guide youth to mark their Bibles during the study to make home study more meaningful.
- Create contests. Let one class, or part of a class, compete against another to see who brings their Bibles most often. Award chocolate.
- Praise those who bring their Bibles. Rather than fussing at those who don't bring their Bible, give attention to those who do.

Do keep extra Bibles in readable translations for youth who do not bring their own. Studying God's Word is more important than whose name is on the inside cover. As their comfort with the Bible increases, youth will more readily turn to their own Bibles.

Q: *I tried an idea from this book and it flopped. What did I do wrong?*

A: Possibly nothing. Some weeks, whatever we try flops. The experiences kids had before arriving, the friends who are there or not there, and the particular mix of the group affects Bible study. To decrease your flop rate:
- Plan more than you need. Then if a central activity flops, you have an alternate.
- Reread an activity that flopped to decide how to alter it next time. Do you need more specific instructions? A different focus? Did the approach not match the type Scripture passage you had?
- Talk to another teacher to find out how she does it.
- Focus on the youth. Let them do most of the doing, talking, creating, reporting.
- Establish firm rules for the learning games right up front. Changing rules frustrates kids. They want games absolutely fair.
- Enjoy the activity yourself. If you like it, youth probably will.

Q: *I'm not creative enough to try all these fancy methods. What can I do that's safe for me?*

A: The only truly creative person is God Himself. He equips all of us to teach. Let Him equip and teach you. In a way, creativity means courage—courage to try something for the sake of your students' learning. I'm woefully inadequate in drama so I frequently skip steps that use it. But one week when I could think of nothing else and was forced to use skits, I discovered that my students loved drama and put complex spiritual truth into understandable form through it.

To expand your creativity, scan a chapter that interests you and try one of the ideas in that chapter. Try just one new method at a time to give yourself time to feel comfortable with it. Step-by-step you can do it.

Q: *My youth get all nervous when I ask them to be creative in their writing or their other assignments.*

A: Because the word "creative" threatens many youth, use phrases like "put your ideas on paper" or "choose your own words." If you use the word "creative," explain that it means "choosing for yourself what you will say, rather than letting someone else decide for you."

Q: *My students are too mature for these creative methods. How can I be sure we stay with the more serious stuff that they say they want?*

A: Creative doesn't mean childish. It means encouraging students to discover and express Bible truth. Before using an activity, notice how it guides youth to dig deeper, discuss in more detail, apply more specifically. Explain this purpose to your students. Some youth may have a parent or former teacher who insists that the only "serious" Bible study is to sit down and listen. Note the many ways Jesus taught (see chapter 1) and show them to your students. Explain before, during, or after a learning experience how it helps you understand the Bible more deeply.

Q: *I feel like I bore the kids. They don't seem to pay much attention. How can I become more interesting to them?*

A: The best cure for boredom is meaningful Bible study applied to young lives. Your church's curriculum should help with this. To help your curriculum or your self-designed sessions become more need-centered:

- Focus on the kids. Find ways to help them talk, draw, express Bible truth. Let them talk more than you do (see chapter 8).
- Notice what works and repeat it, though not too often.
- Invite youth's help in planning the lesson. Telephone a student and offer two possible learning methods. Ask which he prefers. Call another to draw a rebus to put under the concentration game. Invite another to lead a small group, providing directions. Participation helps youth "own" the study and motivates them to make it work.

Q: *I'd love to try all these interesting ideas, but I just don't have time to get them all ready. If I just talk, I don't have to make all the visuals and prepare all the experiences.*

A: Preparing to guide students to study the Bible for themselves usually takes about the same time, sometimes less time, as studying for a lecture. You still begin with your personal Bible study so you understand the passage. But then focus your time on preparing to guide youth rather than deciding what you'll say. Choose a learning activity for each of the four basics: 1. Read the Bible, 2. Discover Bible facts, 3. Understand Bible facts, 4. Apply Bible facts. Consider the preparation needed for this combination:

- **Read:** In script form ("Bible as Script," chapter 4). Preparation: Underline copies of the passage in different colors to cue readers.
- **Discover facts:** Youth will work in pairs to find five Bible facts, create a fact matching game ("Fact Match," chapter 5), and play to reinforce the facts. Preparation: Get markers and 10 cards for each pair.
- **Understand:** Youth will write a letter home about the events in the passage from the perspective of a Bible character ("Letters," chapter 7). Preparation: Get paper and pencils, list characters to give choices.
- **Apply:** Youth will choose one of the facts they wrote for the matching game and make a speech ("30-Second Speech," chapter 8) about how that truth can impact their lives. Preparation: None.

See appendix A for five steps to involvement lesson preparation.

APPENDIX A
Tips for Bible Study Preparation

Whether you're using prepared curriculum or starting from scratch, this R.E.A.D.Y. acrostic summarizes five basic steps for Bible study preparation:

Read the passage first and jot down what it says to you. Your insight is valuable along with that of the teacher who wrote the curriculum.

Examine the Bible passage using the commentary material in your curriculum or by using Bible commentaries or articles.

Assess the needs of your youth. How would Jesus answer your youth's questions? How would He meet the needs they have expressed recently? Seek methods that make the application of the passage obvious.

Decide which learning activities you will use. Choose about four activities: one that guides youth to READ the passage, one that guides them to discover Bible FACTS, one that guides youth to UNDERSTAND the facts, and one that guides them to APPLY the facts to their lives.

Yesterday's lesson becomes tomorrow's life response. What is the one Bible truth you want your class to remember? Repeat it during the session, let your methods demonstrate it, and emphasize it at the end.

Bathe all the above steps in prayer and a request for the Holy Spirit's guidance. As John 16:5-15 explains, the Holy Spirit is the One who convicts, guides, and makes Bible truth clear.

APPENDIX B
Twenty Ways to Divide into Groups

Tired of "one-two; one-two"? Use a different method each time you divide youth into small groups or teams.

1. LAST DIGIT OF PHONE NUMBER: For two groups, put the "odds" in one group and the "evens" in another. For more teams, group several numbers together.

Advantages—Youth want to know each other's phone numbers. They may pay close attention to each other as they divide.

Disadvantages—Groups must be a factor of 10. Groups may be uneven. If this happens, divide again by the second-to-last digit.

2. BIRTH MONTH: Divide youth into 2, 3, 4, 6, or 12 groups by birth month. For three groups, those born in January through April form one group, and so on.

Advantages—Youth are proud of their birthdays. This gives opportunity for lighthearted competition, like "April is the best!"

Disadvantages—Groups may divide unevenly. If this occurs, shuffle by actual birthdate, moving late April to the May group, etc.

3. JAWBREAKERS: Give out jawbreakers to suck on. At group time, direct youth to stick out their tongues. Divide by tongue color.

Advantages—This is neutral and fun. Youth won't suspect the candy as the dividing method.

Disadvantages—Candy causes cavities.

4. HAIR COLOR: Direct the youth to stand in one long line, arranging themselves from light to dark hair. Group "A" is the first four kids in line, group "B" the second four, and so on.

Advantage—You can give compliments about each youth's hair.

Disadvantage—Some people think blonds (or some other color) have more fun and may feel uncomfortable having hair color pointed out. And of course this method doesn't work well if your students all have very similar haircolor.

5. PUZZLE PIECE: Cut paper into the number of people you want in a group. Distribute pieces and direct youth to find others who complete their puzzle.

Advantage—Develops mingling skills.

Disadvantage—Takes time to cut puzzles.

6. TICKETS UNDER CHAIR: Give each student a ticket (any rectangle of paper) on entering. Or place the tickets under chairs before students arrive. To prevent ticket exchanging, give both various shapes and colors so youth don't know the dividing method. Or form groups with one of each color rather than the same colors.

Advantages—Easy to do; many variations. Tickets don't have to be elaborate and can be made at the last minute. For the under-chair variation, students don't know the ticket is there until they sit.

Disadvantages—It takes time to tape all the tickets under all the chairs. Youth can exchange tickets to get in certain groups.

7. CLASS AGAINST CLASS: If you have more than one youth class, announce an end-of-the-session competition.

Advantages—This encourages study and promotes a team feeling in the class. It also encourages cooperation to win.

Disadvantages—One class may be older or smarter than the other. If a loss is handled poorly, one class may feel superior to the other.

8. COLORED PENCILS: Pass out pencils and divide by color.

Advantage—Students won't think of pencils as a group-maker.

Disadvantage—You may not have different colored pencils.

9. MARKED OR COLORED PAPER: Distribute paper. Direct youth to look on the back for their group number. Vary by forming groups by color (all the same or one of each color).

Advantages—Little preparation is needed since you bring paper for many class activities anyway. Can be varied each time it is used.

Disadvantage—Your team activity may not require paper.

10. COLOR OF EYES: Place the blue-eyed youth in one group, the brown-eyed in another, and the green and hazel in another group.

Advantages—It gives a chance to notice and compliment youth's eyes, using such words as "loving eyes," "expressive eyes," "spunky eyes," "happy eyes."

Disadvantages—There may be more of one eye color than another. Some youth may not like the color of their eyes. Some youth may feel self-conscious if their eyes aren't the "standard."

11. SET-UP CHAIRS: If you need four groups of six, cluster the chairs in four circles of six chairs. Youth will group themselves.

Advantages—It is hassle-free and allows you to get right to teaching rather than taking time for dividing into groups.

Disadvantages—Youth may move the chairs. This method may not be helpful if you have a problem with cliques.

12. NOTES IN BALLOONS: Write numbers on small pieces of paper and insert them in uninflated balloons. Direct youth to blow up the balloons and shake them (or pop them) to read the numbers.

Advantage—Balloons add intrigue and color.

Disadvantages—Youth might get distracted by playing with balloons. It also makes a grand mess, can be loud, and takes time to prepare.

13. COLOR OF CLOTHES/SHOES: Look around the room to discover two or three color groups and divide by those. For example, one group might be wearing blue or green; a second group is wearing red or brown. Vary by using shirt or dress color one time, shoe color the next, pants color the next.

Advantage—Youth enjoy being noticed for what they wear.

Disadvantages—Everyone may be wearing the same color. More may be wearing one color than any other color. If so, divide by shade.

14. SHOE SIZE: Instruct youth to recall their shoe size. Direct the odd sizes to one group, even to another, and half sizes to a third. Divide by odd/even, not large/small, to avoid embarrassment.

Advantage—Allows for private response.

Disadvantages—Youth with big feet will feel self-conscious about it. Kids can "cheat."

15. ANIMAL SOUNDS: Write several animal names on your chalkboard. Challenge youth to choose one, make the sound the animal makes, and find other animals of the same kind. Vary it by saying they must form a "barnyard group"—one of each animal. This is best before a team assignment that is active.

Advantages—It's fun. It permits youth to be silly with a purpose. It relieves energy which can then be channeled for Bible study.

Disadvantages—It's noisy. Groups may form unevenly.

16. HEIGHT: Line the group up from shortest to tallest. Divide the line into groups.

Advantages—Shows that height has nothing at all to do with ability. Gives camaraderie between people of similar height.

Disadvantages—Avoid this division with junior high boys, if one boy has not yet grown, or if one girl is taller than the boys.

17. GUYS/GIRLS: Put guys on one team and girls on another.

Advantages—Can demonstrate that guys are as smart as girls and vice versa. Can reduce distracting public displays of affection.

Disadvantages—You may have more girls than boys or vice versa.

18. DIVIDE THE ROOM: Divide youth into groups according to where they are sitting.

Advantages—Youth usually sit next to people they feel comfortable with, so this works well for assignments which require comfort.

Disadvantages—Some friendships are counterproductive to good Bible study. One who must impress another may hesitate to share. Two who try to out-macho each other may refuse to participate.

19. "IF YOU HAVE . . .": Divide those who have done their homework from those who have not. Divide those who have braces from those who do not.

Advantages—This helps youth to get to know each other. Youth will come wondering what you'll think of next. It's unusual and fun.

Disadvantages—Groups may not divide evenly.

20. CHOOSE YOUR OWN GROUP: From time to time, encourage youth to choose their own groups.

Advantages—When youth choose their own groups, they develop friendships, affirm those they choose to be with, and feel accepted.

Disadvantages—When youth choose, they might limit themselves to certain friends or choose distracting or destructive matches.

IMPORTANT: Under no circumstances allow teams to alternate picking individuals. No matter how it is done, someone is chosen last and that person hurts. All youth should feel accepted at church. Refuse to set up a situation that will cause anyone to feel rejected.

APPENDIX C
Twenty-Five Ways to Make Announcements

Announcements happen every week. Keep your kids listening by varying the way you make announcements.

1. ON THE FLOOR: Write your announcements one to a page and display them across the floor.

2. WORD OF MOUTH 1: In this casual version, tell key youth about the event. They will tell others, which convinces the group that "everybody is going."

3. WORD OF MOUTH 2: The formal version is the old-fashioned "telephone." With students seated in a long line or circle, whisper the announcement to the person on one end, who whispers to the next, and so on. Ask the one at the other end to recite it. Shuffle positions and send the next announcement down the line.

4. ON THE CEILING: Youth's eyes continually wander to the ceiling. Take advantage of this by placing announcements there. Vary it by hanging some posters on masking tape strips at various heights.

5. DOOR POSTER: Cover the entire door opening with paper. Write your announcements on it. Attach it at the top only so class members won't break the paper as they come through. VARIATION: Tape the door after youth are in the room. Allow students to break through on their way out.

6. ON STUDENTS: Let kids "wear" announcements as hats, notes on backs, notes on noses, or the old-fashioned "sandwich boards."

7. SECRET MESSAGES: Make a big deal of saying only certain people will get to hear a particular announcement. Slip notes to those involved with the activity. It may be an event just for junior highers or for the youth council, but never an exclusive event.

8. MAPS WITH DETAILS: Write your announcement directly on a hand-drawn map to the location. Write in the corners details such as time, address, and what to bring.

9. CODED MESSAGES: Send a postcard in code or give the coded announcement as youth arrive. The fun of unscrambling focuses youth's attention on the content. Possibilities are endless: If you're announcing a new Bible study series, scramble the titles. If you want to emphasize saving money for the coming retreat, make a treasure map with clues to the treasure. If someone's birthday is coming, encode the date and age.

10. ANSWERING MACHINE: Invest in an answering machine for the church or your home. When youth call, they'll get a different message each week that conveys announcements as well as spiritual growth tips.

11. SINGING COMMERCIAL: Enlist a youth or team of youths to compose and sing a commercial including all your announcements.

12. POSTCARDS AND NEWSLETTERS: Mail or distribute a newsletter with coming events, a challenge to live the Bible truth you're studying, and more. These can fit on a postcard or fill a page. Teenagers love mail.

13. GUESS THE ANNOUNCEMENT: Many announcements are standard (youth choir this afternoon . . .) and youth know what they are. But guessing reminds them. It's a favorite in my group.

14. COMPUTER PRINTOUTS: Many computer printers produce large banners, sometimes in color, that make great eye-catching ways to post announcements. Vary the way you display them to maintain interest: horizontal, vertical, upside down, in pieces, as a puzzle to assemble.

15. FOOTPRINTS: Write one word to a footprint and let youth enjoy walking on them as they read.

16. TAPE RECORDER: Youth play the announcements as they enter. Make it more intriguing by varying the voice each week.

17. SCAVENGER HUNT: Put one announcement at each discovery location.

18. PEEK-AND-VIEW BOX: Amazingly, youth love this one. Attach announcements inside the box and cut two eye holes and slits for light.

19. DIFFERENT YOUTH: Invite a different youth to give the announcement each week. He or she can prepare a skit, a song, or simply tell the announcements with interest. Varying the voice invites attention.

20. DOORKNOB HANGERS: Put these on the doorknob of your classroom, deliver them to youth homes, or distribute and direct youth to hang them on their bedroom doors at home.

21. PHOTOGRAPHS: Display photographs of the last Bible study activity or trip. Seeing what a good time the group had motivates others to come. Prepare a poster or pass the photographs with the date, time, and place on the back.

22. SKIT: Guide two or more youth to prepare and present a skit that communicates the announcements.

23. PRINTED PENCILS OR BALLOONS: If your event is several weeks away, order pencils, balloons, or other "printables" printed with the date, time, place and purpose.

24. T-SHIRT: Print T-shirts prior to a retreat or other big Bible study event and require youth to wear them for admission. Distributing the shirts ahead of time increases the possibility that youth will attend.

25. BUTTONS: Use black stickers on white name tags cut in the shape of your theme. Write the details on them. Wear them.

BIRTHDAYS: Though not a technique, this announcement should be a part of every week. Keep a chronological list of youth's birthdays and weekly note who has a birthday coming. Sing, hug, or otherwise congratulate these people.

APPENDIX D
Alphabetical Listing of Learning Activities

See an activity in your curriculum you're not sure how to do? Remember a method from this book but can't remember which chapter it is in? This listing of activities and topics can solve both dilemmas. The ideas in each chapter are also listed alphabetically for your convenience.